THE COACHMAKERS

The Coachmakers

A HISTORY OF THE WORSHIPFUL COMPANY OF
COACHMAKERS
AND COACH HARNESS MAKERS
1677–1977

Edited by HAROLD NOCKOLDS

J. A. ALLEN : LONDON & NEW YORK

ISBN 0 85131 270 5

Published in 1977 by J. A. Allen & Company Limited,
1 Lower Grosvenor Place,
Buckingham Palace Road,
London, SW1W 0EL.
and at
Canaan,
New York 12029,
United States of America.

Book production by Bill Ireson.

Typeset in 11 on 13 pt Monotype Ehrhardt
by HBM Typesetting Limited, Chorley, Lancashire.
Printed and bound by Redwood Burn Limited, Trowbridge and Esher.

Foreword

By Lt.-Col. Sir John Miller, K.C.V.O., D.S.O., M.C.

YOUNG by the standards of the City of London and some of its senior Livery Companies, the Coachmakers and Coach Harness Makers nevertheless reached their 300th year on 31st May 1977. The granting of their Charter by King Charles II in 1677 did not mark the beginning of coachmaking but rewarded and gave Royal recognition to a craft and trade which for at least 100 years had been " . . . . beneficial to the Noblemen of our Kingdom and other our subjects."

With the arrival of the motor car in this century the craft gradually declined, and the coachmakers of the past have been succeeded in the Livery Company by their counterparts of modern times, the manufacturers of motor cars and aeroplanes (the coaches of the air).

But interest in horse-drawn vehicles has not died. The Tercentenary of the Coachmakers is a cause for satisfaction not only to the Company but to the increasing number of people who have recaptured the pleasure of driving, all of whom owe their enjoyment in part to the splendid vehicles made in such profusion by the coachmakers of the last century. To meet their needs a growing number of businesses are now at work around the country restoring old vehicles and making replicas of old designs with modern materials and techniques, and in some cases carriages of a completely novel design.

Horse-drawn vehicles in great variety are kept at the Royal Mews, where a party of members of the Company and their wives were invited in November 1976 to witness the horses being put to the coaches and carriages taking part in the procession from Buckingham Palace to Westminster for the State Opening of Parliament by Her Majesty the Queen.

For the visitors the routine of stable and coach-house, followed by the sight and sound of nine coaches and carriages – some driven from the box, others by postillion – as they circled the courtyard several times before moving off to the Palace, brought to life the period when coachmakers and their craft were at the height of their powers.

5

On view in the surrounding coach-houses were many other vehicles – most of them made by past members of the Livery – ranging from the huge Gold State Coach of 1762 to barouches, broughams and landaus down to a little closed pony carriage and a pair of governess carts. Superb sets of harness, representing the second activity of the Company, were also to be seen.

The vehicles in the Royal Mews are no mere museum pieces. They are working vehicles in regular use, as are the four-in-hand private drags of the Coaching Club and the phaetons, wagonettes, gigs and dog-carts owned by members of the British Driving Society – now nearly 2,000 strong.

This book tells the 300 years' history of an institution that is of the very essence of our national heritage. It links us in thought with the craftsmen of bygone days whose magnificent products we admire – and still use.

I deem it an honour to have been made a member of this Company, and may the Worshipful Company of Coachmakers and Coach Harness Makers – and all that it stands for – long continue to prosper and to fulfil the needs of the "road", whatever they may be.

JOHN MILLER*

*Lt.-Col. Sir John Miller is the Crown Equerry. He is responsible for the Royal Mews Department and all matters concerned with travel by road, including the motor cars and all the royal horses except those in the thoroughbred studs and racing stables.

Sir John Miller is President of the Coaching Club, a Vice-President of the British Driving Society, and is himself one of Britain's leading whips.

Contents

CONTENTS

List of Illustrations

Introduction

By Maurice Smith, D.F.C.

THIS book, published to mark the tercentenary of the Coachmakers and Coach Harness Makers, is more than a history of that Worshipful Company, for it traces the growth and decline of the craft from the earliest coaches and carriages of the 17th-century to the replacement of the horse-drawn vehicle by the motor car in modern times.

In re-living those early years of our historic Company we are reminded of the value of apprenticeship as a means of developing skills and pride in a craft, and of safeguarding standards of workmanship and materials in provident times when individual people regarded such matters highly.

Happily the appreciation of those standards is not dead, and we see how a number of small firms are today restoring old carriages, building "new" ones, and restoring fine motor cars.

This book is largely the work of Harold Nockolds, the Company's honorary historian, who has written much of it and edited the whole. Several chapters are reproduced from an earlier history published privately in 1938 on the direction of Lord Iliffe during his Mastership, including Chapter 14 on the Company's plate written by past-Master the Rev. H. G. Rosedale. The revival of horse-drawn carriage building and the restoration of old motor cars are described in Chapters 17 and 18 written by Peter Garnier, chairman of the Livery Committee. Chapter 19 on harness and harness making was contributed by Anthony Hussey of Connolly Brothers (Curriers), with additional material made available by John Richards of Horsedrawn Carriages Limited.

Our special thanks are due to Mr. and Mrs. Sanders Watney, in his case for overseeing Chapter 16 on the growing popularity of driving, in which he has played a leading part, and to Marylian Watney, the acknowledged authority on the history of carriages and coaches, for her unstinted advice and help.*

MAURICE SMITH
Master, 1977

*Further acknowledgements are given on page 230.

13

1 The Meaning of the Livery

THOSE who know all about Livery Companies and what they stand for may choose to skip this chapter. But there are others – especially those who are about to become liverymen – who may like to learn something of the role and traditions of Livery Companies in general, before reading the history of one of them in particular.

The City of London gave birth to its first Livery Company some 600 years ago – which makes the 300 years old Worshipful Company of Coachmakers and Coach Harness Makers seem a comparative youngster. Other British cities and towns, like Canterbury, Edinburgh, York, Glasgow, Bristol, Preston and Norwich also have Livery traditions and the movement has its foreign counterparts in Germany, France, Belgium and Switzerland. But nowhere has the idea continued to flourish more vigorously than in the City of London.

Livery Companies were formed for a variety of reasons – religious, trade and fraternal. The religious connection came from the concentration of certain trades around the numerous churches in the City of London. The early brotherhoods and fraternities at these churches were the basis of the later Livery Companies. For example, the Brotherhood of St. Clement's at the church of St. Lawrence Jewry became the Founders' Company and another fraternity at the same church grew into the Girdlers' Company. The Haberdashers' Company was originally called the Fraternity of St. Catherine the Virgin of Haberdashers in the City of London.

In the course of time the trades became dispersed and their connection with individual churches largely disappeared. Today a few companies hold a short service in a neighbouring city church before their Livery dinners, but the most important religious link for Livery Companies as a whole is the Annual United Service of the Guilds of the City of London held at St. Paul's Cathedral. The spectacle of a score of Masters of various Companies followed by dignitaries of the Corporation and the Church – the Sheriffs, the Court of Aldermen, the Lord Bishop of London and the Lord

15

Mayor himself bringing up the rear – all dressed in their many coloured liveries, robes and vestments and proceeding slowly up the chancel of the resplendent cathedral, is a stirring prelude to the service, which itself is a memorable witness to the enduring life of the great City of London.*

The trade element, originally the keystone of the Livery Company structure, has inevitably altered in line with changes in industry and commerce. There are few Bowyers and Fletchers nowadays, because bows and arrows have gone out of fashion as weapons of war. Nor is it easy to find many Fanmakers, Loriners and Wax Chandlers, but these Companies still flourish with modern versions of the old crafts and trades forming the nuclei of the Liveries. The Coachmakers and Coach Harness Makers provide a good example of this metamorphosis, the present day equivalents of the founders being the manufacturers of motor cars, aeroplanes and their components.

Naturally there have been casualties. Some Companies have ceased to exist altogether and others have been absorbed by near relatives. They include some pleasantly named ones – the Virginals Makers' Company, the Galoche Makers', the Hatband Makers' and the Heaumers' (makers of shoulder length armoured helmets).

Nevertheless, there are still some 80 separate Livery Companies in London. The oldest is the Mercers' Company (founded 1394) and the youngest the Scientific Instrument Makers' (founded 1963). By an act of the Court of Aldermen in 1515, the official number of each Company was "sette, ordeyned and agreed", the Mercers' heading the list followed by the rest of the 12 "great Companies" in order of precedence – the Grocers', Drapers', Fishmongers', Goldsmiths', Merchant Taylors' and Skinners', Haberdashers', Salters', Ironmongers' and Vintners'. Both the Merchant Taylors' Company and the Skinners' claimed sixth place; this argument was settled by the Lord Mayor who ruled that they should take turn and turn about in sixth and seventh places.

The Coachmakers' Company (No. 72) is one of the last of the old City Guilds, for after the Fanmakers' (No. 76) were formed in 1709 (receiving their charter in 1809) there was an interval of almost 200 years before another new Company, the Solicitors', came into being in 1908 (receiving their charter in 1944).

*A fuller account of that life, together with brief descriptions of the individual Livery Companies, is given by John Kennedy Melling in *London's Guilds and Liveries*, published in paperback by Shire Publications. The editor is indebted to the author of that booklet for some of the facts mentioned in this chapter.

16

The Companies were also allotted their own colours, the Coachmakers' being given blue and yellow.

The early procedures and disciplines entailed by membership of the Livery, as practised by the Coachmakers', are described in later chapters. Here it may be said that the system of indentures, or the binding of apprentices, was an important part of the Livery's business and was firmly controlled because it ensured adequate training and good workmanship. The Livery controlled not only the conduct of the apprentices but the liverymen who took them on – they were responsible for supplying the apprentices with meat, drink, clothing and the other necessities of life. Cases of poor workmanship and neglect of apprentices resulted in the offending liveryman being fined by the Court of Assistants at their regular meetings, usually held in the Company's own Hall. It is perhaps worth recalling that the word "livery" means not only the distinctive clothing formerly worn by members of the City Companies, but also the provision of food and drink served out to retainers. Nowadays, livery gowns are worn only by the Master and Wardens on official occasions. Since 1761, gowns have been made of mazarine (a deep, rich, blue) silk with fur trimmed sleeves. Charity and good works have always been a dominant activity of the Livery Companies, taking many different forms according to the funds at the Companies' disposal. Of equal importance has been the Companies' contribution to education. Again, the effort has been varied and the Coachmakers' pioneer work in this area is described in the pages which follow.

In earlier times the Livery Companies were called upon by some monarchs to supply cash for ships, sailors, soldiers and arms to meet national emergencies. In the South African War, the Coachmakers contributed cash towards the cost of equipping the City Imperial Volunteers. This interest in the armed forces has been revived in recent times, the Coachmakers' Company having "adopted" a ship of the Royal Navy, a regiment of the Army and a squadron of the Royal Air Force.

The Court of the Coachmakers' Company meets four times a year, followed by a Court dinner. The remaining members of the Company are freemen of the Livery who, after being appropriately proposed and seconded by members of the Court, have been admitted by servitude, patrimony or redemption (purchase). The applicant takes the oath of loyalty at a meeting of the Court and receives the certificate of the freedom of the Livery. He then presents this to the Chamberlain of the Corporation of London for the brief ceremony of being made a freeman of the City of London. Taking another oath of loyalty and signing the Roll are followed by a handshake, and the freedom is presented in a red case. Once in possession of the freedom of the City, the freeman of the Company can apply to become a liveryman. Promotion to the Court is by seniority and by the same process through the degrees of Wardens to Master.

Three Livery dinners are held by the Coachmakers at intervals during the year. At the first dinner after his election, the choice of official guests is customarily the prerogative of the Master. At the other dinners, guests are usually chosen to represent a particular aspect of public life; such as a profession, one of the armed forces, an industry or a sport.

Most people think of the City Livery Companies as an essentially masculine society, though in fact women are entitled to apply for the freedom of a Company, or the freedom of the City of London (indeed, the Queen is a freeman of the City). Women used to appear frequently on the rolls of Livery Companies and there are a few today in certain Companies.

The Coachmakers have had only one woman member, the Baroness Burdett-Coutts, to whom the Court offered the freedom of the Livery in 1894 in recognition of her generous assistance to the craft of coachmaking in providing a training course for students.

For centuries, liverymen of the City Companies had the right to vote for the four Members of Parliament who stood for the City of London. This was a political privilege given them in exchange for their oath of loyalty and fidelity to the King and his lawful successors, but in 1918 this franchise was restricted to those liverymen with business premises qualifications. In 1947 the register of such voters, 740 in all, was abolished.

Nevertheless, the Livery Companies are still privileged to attend the democratic processes of the Corporation of London, being represented by their Masters and selected liverymen at Common Hall on Midsummer Day and Michaelmas Day, when the elections of the Sheriffs and the Lord Mayor of London are held at Guildhall. On receiving the precept of the Clerk of the Company, the selected liverymen (who must be freemen and liverymen of at least one year's service) enter Guildhall after passing through a barrier in the courtyard guarded by the various Company beadles. Common Hall begins with a procession of the Masters of the Livery Companies, the Aldermen and their beadles, the officers of the Corporation, the Lord Mayor and the Sheriffs. Only liverymen are entitled to attend Common Hall for the elections which follow, though their wives may sit at the back as guests.

2 Origin and Early History

WHAT actually was the first use of the coach in England does not greatly matter; that will remain in dispute. But we do know that the mother of King Richard II rode in a "whirlicote" when she accompanied him to Mile End, there to parley with the rebels in the Peasants' Revolt of 1381.

King Henry VIII is said to have astonished the Londoners of his day by making his victorious entry after Bosworth Field in a lumbering contraption on wheels drawn by a large number of horses. Mary Tudor rode through the City of London to West-minster on the day before her Coronation in 1553, sitting in a chariot drawn by six horses. Her sister, Elizabeth, and the Lady Anne of Cleeves were in a second chariot-and-six and there were a third and fourth in the glittering procession.

The first coach produced in England is thought to have been supplied by Walter Rippon to the Earl of Rutland in 1555. Rippon made a second coach for Mary Tudor the following year.

But it was Mary Tudor's sister, Elizabeth I, who can be said to have inaugurated the coach's popularity when, in 1560, she received a massive specimen from Holland. This was reported to be a gift from William Boonen, who became her coachman. The occasions when she showed herself to her loyal people in this great equipage were so successful that in 1564 Walter Rippon was asked to produce the first State coach, which Elizabeth subsequently used at the opening of Parliament in 1571. It must have looked all the more impressive as it was the only vehicle in the procession!

Hofnagel's painting of the Nonsuch Palace, dated 1582, with the Queen riding in the foreground, shows the State coach as a large, square, vehicle with a "boot" – a projection at each side in which passengers or attendants might sit, with their backs to the carriage itself. Another detail of its design is revealed in a courtier's des-cription of the Queen's visit to Warwick, when she "caused every part and side of her coach to be opened, that all her subjects present might behold her, which most gladly they desired".

The State coach of Queen Elizabeth I, its gracious owner raised high upon cushions to cheer the sight of all, set a fashion which the more wealthy of the aristocracy were quick to take up. The cost of a coach in use at that time is indicated in the household book of the Kitson family:

> *1573.* For my master's coach, with all the furniture thereto belonging, except horses, £34. 14s. For the painting of my master's and my mistress' arms upon the coach, 2s. 6d. For the coach horses bought of Mr. Paxton, £11. 13s. 3d.

The town coach of the early Stuarts was a heavy, cumbersome affair, carrying four passengers and being drawn by two, or four, or sometimes even six, heavy horses. The coach body was square, suspended by great leather straps at the four corners from upright posts which sprang from the axle trees. A cross-bar joining the two forward posts gave the driver an uneasy and perilous seat; his feet rested on the carriage pole. The box seat was covered with a hammer cloth*, embellished with the armorial bearings of the noble owner, which were also painted on the doors. At first the plaything of men and women of rank, the coach, despite its weight and inconvenience, grew in popular favour and by 1625 hackney coaches were established in London. These were often the cast-off vehicles of the rich, in which state they quickly became shabby and dirty and were accordingly despised.

To begin with the hackney† coaches did not ply for hire but were kept in jobbing yards. A smaller and narrower new type appeared, called "hackney hell carts" by ribald detractors, while Bishop Hall indignantly called them "sin guilty".

By 1635, some 50 hackney coaches were allowed to ply for hire, being challenged by sedan chairs which had been introduced a year earlier by Sir Sanders Duncomb. The congestion caused in the narrow streets of London by these two hostile factions was such that in 1650, when there were over 300 coaches of all kinds in London, the first traffic jam was recorded.

At the Restoration in 1660, a Royal Proclamation described hackney coaches as a "common nuisance" and forbade their use in London "except to travel three miles out of same".

*The origin of the term "hammer cloth" has often been discussed. J. O. H. Norris believed it was derived from "hammock" because the driver's seat was hammock-shaped. *English Country Life 1780–1830* by E. W. Bovill quoted *The Servants' Guide for 1830* as stating "the box was originally called the hamper, or box in which, in the early days of family coaches, provisions were carried." From this Mrs. Marylian Watney advances the plausible suggestion that the cloth covering the box was called the "hamper cloth", which in time was corrupted to "hammer cloth."

†The words "hackney" and "coach" both have Continental roots. Hackney from the French *haquence*, a horse for hire; coach from Kotze, or Kocs, in Hungary where the vehicle is believed to have originated.

The sedan chairs were not the only rivals of the coaches. There were also the watermen, who had previously enjoyed a virtual monopoly of transporting people in the city. They had their own poet, John Taylor:

> *Carroaches, coaches, jades, and Flanders mares*
> *Doe rob us of our shares, our wares, our fares.*
> *Against the ground we stand and knock our heels,*
> *Whilst all our profit runs away on wheels.*

Taylor lived during the reign of King Charles I. The fair sex, he wrote, had been wont to take a boat and air themselves upon the river, but now . . . .

> . . . . every Gill Turntripe, Mistress Fumkins, Madam Polecat and My Lady Trash, Froth the tapster, Bill the tailor, Lavender the broker, Whiff the tobacco seller and their companion trugs must all be coach'd to St. Albans, Burntwood, Hockey-in-the-Hole, Croydon, Windsor, Uxbridge and many other places.

Taylor gibes at the coaches, as boxes in which people were "tost, tumbled, rumbled and jumbled without mercy". That infernal swarm of vehicles on the roads, he growled, was ruining the watermen's livelihood.

The picture was exaggerated. Samuel Pepys' diary, written between 1660 and 1670, shows that the Thames still served that age as London's chief highway.

It was during the reign of King Charles I that the many different crafts which participate in the building of a coach began drawing together. Already the more eager minds were thinking of establishing themselves as a guild. The Wheelwrights led the movement, fittingly, for nothing in coachbuilding is older than the wheel and the axle, together perhaps the most useful of man's inventions.

Petition was made to the Court of Aldermen at Guildhall in 1631, setting out the advantages which would be gained by trade incorporation. The Aldermen were in no hurrying mood. It was March 1632 when their committee, to whom the matter had been referred, presented a report. Coachmakers were named jointly with Wheelwrights; the original intention evidently was to make one Company for the two trades. The committee found . . . .

> . . . . that many fraudes and deceipts are duly used by Wheelewrights and Coachmakers which doe use in their workes much yonge & unseasoned Tymber, which when it is fitted for wheeles or framed for Coaches doe shrink and thereby being disioynted both Coach and wheeles quickly decaye, whereby men's occasions in their iornys are disapoynted, & their lives many tymes endaungered. Wee finde alsoe that much deale wood in joynt worke of Coaches is used, which breaketh with the shaking of the Coach, and that these abuses, by reason that the said Coaches and Wheeles are paynted and collered, cannot easily be discovered but by one of those facultys nor be reformed but by some politick constitucon prohibiting the same. And wee finde alsoe that many greene wheeles are vended by Bargemen and others which doe often breake in the Streets of the Citty and places adiacent, to the damage and hurte of passengeres.

Such abuses harmed both the public and the trade. The petitioners desired a favourable report from the Aldermen to assist them in procuring Letters Patent from the King for their incorporation. Accordingly, the committee had called joiners, smiths and other craftsmen concerned to give their opinion. All agreed that to make the petitioners a corporation would be the best way to secure reform. This course received approval from the Court of Aldermen, providing that the Company so set up . . . .

> . . . . shall not molest or compel any person whatsoever free of any Company within this Citty using the trade of a wheelwright or coachmaker to be translated into their corporation.

There was also the usual proviso that the ordinances should have the Court of Aldermen's approval. The blacksmith's were not to be restrained from placing ironwork upon the wheels, as they had been accustomed to`do.

On 10th January 1633 the matter was again considered and again referred to a committee, and there it rested, possibly because of some difference of opinion between wheelwrights and coachmakers. Soon the political troubles of the times and the approach of the Civil War made any new project of incorporation impossible.

It was about this time, or a few years later, that the stage coach made its appearance – at first only in the summer. But, so long as the coach remained the primitive vehicle of the first half of the 17th-century, – massively built, heavy, and on the awful roads of the time, frequently immovable – it could never be widely used. Joan Parkes, in *Travel in England in the Seventeenth Century*, points out that although the stage coach was cumbersome and jolting and far from being watertight, it was nevertheless . . . .

. . . . an invention of inestimable benefit for those unable to stand the rigours of horseback.

She went on:

It is true the benefit might not always be apparent. To a woman or child sick in pain, tossing over cobbled streets; to the mother of an infant crying with convulsive energy over twenty miles or more of rough country road – one such child, to save its life, had to be left en route in the course of a long journey – to the traveller left stranded on the roadside ten miles from a town in a coach tipped sideways from the breaking of an axle, or with wheels sunk deep in a quagmire; to these it might seem but a new form of torture. Yet it entailed neither the exposure nor the physical strain inseparable from the old-style travelling. As to peril, it made little difference which method of transit was adopted, so long as the coachman and postillion were sober and cautious. This, as may be imagined, they were not always.

About 1650 great improvements in coach building in England began to be introduced. Men could turn their attention from the distractions of civil war to useful inventions. The coach – and the carriage – became practically suited to the needs of road loco-motion; the roads themselves, unhappily, were little better. An ill-fitting door had replaced the early leather flaps which gave protection of sorts at the entrance from rain and wind. A glass window in the door was next substituted for the upper part of the leather flap, which for a time had been retained. The "glass coach" arrived. By 1662 stage coaches were running regularly between London and York, Chester, Oxford, Dover and Ports-mouth.

The greatest improvement of all was in the suspension of the carriage body. The provision of steel springs – known by 1670 but not regularly used until the next century – effectively reduced jolting and vibration and, by enabling a lighter vehicle to be built, served both the comfort and the purse of the owner and relieved the burden upon the horses. The Royal Society, then newly founded by Charles II, gave great help in the development of the light carriage in the latter half of the 18th-century by encouraging new designs and experiments with springs.

Samuel Pepys patronised the watermen when Navy business called him to Westminster, but at times – very discontentedly – he took a hired coach:

> In the evening (10th July 1668) with my people in a glass hackney-coach to the park, but was ashamed to be seen.

PLATE I

A massive, yet somehow elegant, town coach of the early 18th-century illustrated in a contemporary coachmaker's catalogue presented to the Coachmakers' Company by George Thrupp (Master, 1883).

By the next year the diarist felt sufficiently established and wealthy to realise his ambition to own a chariot of his own. On May Day, Mr. and Mrs. Pepys set out in the new equipage to ride and take the air among the quality:

> At noon home to dinner, and there find my wife extraordinarily fine, with her flowered tabby gown that she made two years ago, now laced exceedingly pretty; and, indeed, was fine all over, and mighty earnest to go, though the day was very lowring, and she would have me put on my fine suit, which I did. And so anon we went alone through the town with our new liveries of serge, and the horses' manes and tails tied with red ribbons, and the standards there gilt with varnish, and all clean, and green reines, that people did mightily look upon us; and the truth is I did not see any coach more pretty, though more gay than ours, all the day . . . . The Park full of coaches, but dusty and windy and cold.

What gave offence to Pepys was that "there were so many hackney coaches as spoiled the sight of the gentlemen's". We know that Pepys gave £50 at Smithfield Horse Market for his fine pair of blacks.

A consideration which perhaps influenced Pepys in his decision to buy a carriage of his own was the greater freedom to move in the City along the streets that had just been widened after the Great Fire of London in 1666.

Another by-product of that disaster was that the coachmakers took advantage of the widened streets to build rather bigger vehicles to replace the large number destroyed in the fire.

3 The Charter Granted – and Surrendered

WITH the return of luxury and extravagance to the town at the Restoration, the body of coachmakers again gave thought to a charter for their growing industry.

The wheelwrights had gone ahead by securing a charter for themselves granted by King Charles II in 1671. There must have been regret that the opportunity of obtaining unity in a single City Company for both trades was missed. A few years had yet to pass before the coachmakers were able to put their case for a charter effectively.

By September 1676, after inspection of the charters of other Companies, a model charter for the coachmakers was drafted. It was submitted to Sir William Jones, the Attorney-General, for his advice. There were a good many people to be paid. Six guineas went to Sir William for his advice; another five guineas as he reported to the King. The Secretary took six guineas "for obtayneing the King's hand" and a first (and not last) fee of £50 was required by the Clerk of Patents; the Recorder of London had a modest two guineas for services given, but the Lord Chancellor's clerk drew five guineas. The outcome of this, and other, expenditure was the Charter, now in the possession of the Company and in the safe-keeping of Guildhall. Altogether the Coachmakers were involved in the expenditure of £250 costs in obtaining it.

The Charter is written in English and bears the date 31st May 1677. The writing covers four large vellum sheets and the head of King Charles II appears in vignette in the initial letter of the richly decorated and illuminated document.

The full Charter is printed in Appendix A. The usual form is followed:

> Arts, trades and misteries of coach making are of antiquity, and of great use and beneficial.to the noble-men of Our Kingdom and Other subjects. Inexpert and

unskilful persons have obtruded. Those knowledgeable in the trade have petitioned for incorporation. The King accordingly doth constitute that Edmund Aubry, our coachmaker, Charles Nevill, our coach harness maker, Thomas Bringham, coachmaker to Our dear brother the Duke of York and others named, and all who follow the trade, are a body politic and corporate in deed and in name as the Master, Wardens, Assistants and Commonalty of the Company of Coachmakers and Coach Harness Makers of London.

The Company had authority to purchase and dispose of lands to the value of £300, besides the Common Hall; to plead and be impleaded in law; to have a seal; to possess a Clerk and a Beadle; with power of search after obtaining a Warrant from the Lord Chief Justice of the King's Bench and, if accompanied by a Constable, the Master, Wardens and Assistants may enter "shopps, Cellars, Sollars, Stables, Coach-houses and suspected places" and examine coaches and materials and find out defects and prosecute offenders. The area of jurisdiction was defined as London and Westminster and the country within twenty miles around.

A Master, three Wardens, and 23 Assistants were to constitute the Court; election day was the 1st September each year. They were empowered to make laws for regulating the trade, impose fines for breaches, and levy distress. No persons, other than freemen of the Company, were allowed to follow the trade. Apprentices had to be bound only to a master who was free of the Company.

The Charter names William Bussey as the first Master; James Page, James Masters and Stephen Phillips as Wardens, and among the Assistants named are the King's coachmaker and coach harness maker and the Duke of York's coachmaker. The Company started proudly.

Immediately following the receipt of the foundation Charter a set of Ordinances were drawn up and approved, as required by law, at a cost of £121. A number were concerned with the election of the ruling body, others with apprenticeship. The term was to be for not less than seven, or more than nine, years. All members of the Court and the Livery might take two apprentices, freemen of the Company one only. The "foreigner" (non-freeman) was

excluded from the trade. The Ordinances deal minutely with administration, discipline, finance and search. Nothing seemed too small for mention. Thus, No. 8 lays it down that "no member be suffered to eat, drink, or take tobacco during the sitting of the Court, but that such person who shall desire the same shall withdraw out of the Court Room".

29

PLATE 2
Two loving cups presented to the Company in its early days: (left) date mark 1650, maker Andrew Moore, given by Samuel Aubrey in 1677 (see page 159); (right) date mark 1709, maker Humphrey Payne, given in 1710 by Edmond Aubrey.

An Assistant is enjoined to speak when required, or to desist from speech when ordered by the Master, and "use, endeavour, and keep all decent order and behaivour in Court", under a penalty of 3s. 4d. Again, the order in which the Court sits is to be "as they stand named and in order in the Charter", the penalty for non-compliance being 5s.

New material entirely must be used in a new coach made for general sale; but in the case of one "bespoke by any particular person" who desired some material or fittings of his own to be used, such employment of second-hand material was allowed if the buyer knew all about it and freely consented.

PLATE 3
This small tankard with cover, date mark 1676 – still owned by the Company – was given by William Fowler on 1st September 1677. Fowler was elected Master in 1686. (See page 161).

In the last years of his reign King Charles II, with his father's fate before his eyes, sought again a Royal autocracy. That the attempt failed is a matter of history. The attack did not fall upon the nation's representatives in Parliament. Less formidable opponents were chosen, the corporations of the country. The municipal bodies must be made subservient to the King's will and to that of his Ministers. They were required, under the Writ of *Quo Warranto*, to surrender their Charters – by a lawyer's quibble – misuse of powers being alleged. In return they received other charters, which extinguished old liberties and left the Royal Court free to eject Mayor, Aldermen and officers of the electors' choice and to put in their place its own creatures.

The Corporation of London at Guildhall fought stubbornly, but by judgement of the King's Bench Court it went down. Eight London Aldermen were turned out and their seats filled by the King's placemen; the King himself nominated the Lord Mayor. The Recorder of London, Sir John Treby, who had advised against a surrender, was summarily dismissed.

Obviously, the City Companies were the next target. They, too, could be reduced to subservience. The intention of the Crown was announced with brutal frankness. What should they do? When the powerful Corporation of the City of London could not stand up against the King and the Judges, the Companies' chance in a fight was hopeless. Most of them forestalled receipt of the Writ of *Quo Warranto*, with all its harassing proceedings and costs, by voluntarily surrendering their Charters. The Coachmakers and Coach Harness Makers were one Company who did this.

Unfortunately, there is a gap in the records of the Company at this important stage. The Orders of the Court from 1680 to 1687 have been lost, but we are not without information.

King Charles II left this world of trouble on the 6th February 1685, apologising for being such an unconscionable time in dying. His unpopular brother, the Duke of York, ruled as James II. The policy was Charles' and although James' name and authority were used in the new Charter, it is probable that he had little to do with preparing and carrying out the attack on the City Companies. On the 5th October 1686, the Coachmakers Company surrendered to the King the powers conferred by Charter. "And do" it was said "with all submission impore his grace and favour to regrant the same, or as many of them" as in James's great

31

wisdom should seem most conducive to the good government of the Company.

The Coachmakers had an *Advocatus Diaboli* in the camp, a man named John Bradford, who had never held any office. A solicitor by profession, he made himself very busy, for his own ends, in bringing about the destruction of the liberties of the Company and hanging around its neck the second Charter of 1687, with all its restrictions.

The charges laid against him are set out in a paper at Guildhall called "Mr. Bradford's Case".* One Burton figures as a willing collaborator:

> He procured Mr. Burton to threaten the Company that if they did not surrender their Charter the King would bring a *Quo Warranto* against them, whereupon a Court of Assistants was called, and upon a long debate of the matter they did agree a surrender of the Charter upon hopes of haveing diverse additions in their new Charter as was promised (tho' not at all performed). After the surrender was sealed, a list of certaine of the old Members was made and agreed upon to be inserted in the new Charter by diverse of the old Court of assistants, and delivered to one of the then Lord Chancellor's gentlemen, which list was after altered, contrary to those Assistants' knowledge or approbacon, by Bradford being a Solicittor with Burton, and diverse young members placed therein above those that had been their senior Members, & other persons that were never of the Assistants before placed before old Members that had been Masters & Wardens.

Bradford, never having been a Steward, never having paid a fine on admission to the Livery, or been an Assistant, not having served as Under Warden – he possessed every disqualification – was incapable, under the Company's law, of holding high office.

Nevertheless, "managing the whole affair with Mr. Burton", he got himself named Upper Warden in the Charter of King James II and acted as Upper Warden in the new regime that it set up.

*Guildhall Miscellaneous Documents: Companies, 2–1.

This second Charter, of James II, is dated 12th May 1687. It was received by the new Master, named Benjamin Thody, who on the 1st June met the three Wardens at the house in Creed Lane of Brian Courthope, the Clerk, where the oaths were taken.

The first Court under the Charter assembled at the Jewell Chamber in Guildhall six days later, when the document was read. As the Charter had short shrift, it need not be studied here. The chief change made – a sufficient one – was that the King, by Order in Council, might displace or remove the Master, Wardens, Assistants and Clerk, or any of them, requiring the Company to proceed to new elections. The new men were liable to be removed in the same manner. To this outrage the Company was forced to submit.

The immediate effect was that William Fowler, the elected Master, was ejected for Thody; three Charter Wardens, with Bradford as their senior, took the place of the elected Wardens and eight or nine Assistants were thrown out. Eleven new Assistants were placed on the Court. On election day, 1st September 1687, Bradford put himself in nomination for Master but was not returned, Thody being re-elected. Bradford had his ambition next year, 1688, when he defeated Thody and took his place as Master.

Bradford's reign was short. James II had his own troubles. A few weeks after Bradford's elections, King James, hoping to gain the goodwill of the City of London which he so badly needed, made a regrant to the Companies of their surrendered rights; and the *Quo Warranto* proceedings were wiped out, wholly and effectively, when William and Mary came to the throne.

Mr. Fowler, whose term had been broken, was restored to the Master's chair, the ejected Wardens again took up their offices, old members of the Court of Assistants came back to place and precedence.

There was no nomination of Bradford for any office. As a last gesture of ill-will, he refused to deliver up King James's Charter and the Company's registers and other books which had been in his custody. The Master, and three others, were charged to interview the Lord Mayor and to seek redress. On mature consideration, John Bradford capitulated, restored the Company's Charter and books and, thereafter, he disappears.

33

These disturbances of the normal order had a curious effect upon the Livery. Doubt was entertained in some quarters as to whether or not there was a Livery! Certainly, a Livery had been granted by the Court of Aldermen on the 12th July 1687, two months after the new Charter was given. But what was the position now?

Again, the Company went to the Court of the Aldermen, asking to have the matter made clear. Fortunately, the Aldermen had no misgivings after receiving the report of their committee. That report, made in October 1694, recalled that after the original grant of Livery in Sir John Peake's Mayoralty, the Company was summoned . . . .

> . . . . to the eleccon of Lord Major, Sherriffs, and other Officers 9 October 1688 in their Liveries. Also the 2 October 1691 they were againe summoned to give in the names of their Livery in order to a scrutiny of a poll then taken. Further we find them summoned againe 22 October 1691 to attend in their Gownes the Lord Major to Westminster and back againe, & 25 October 1692 againe summoned as a Livery Company to attend the Lord Major to Westminster and back againe upon the Lord Major's day, as other Livery Companys does; so that upon the whole matter we humbly conceive they are still a Livery Company and ought to be summoned to the said eleccons as formerly they were.

Accordingly, the Court of Aldermen established and allowed the Coachmakers Company a Livery and clothing; and no question of the right has since arisen.

In the days when gifts to those in high places who were able to help things along were quite usual, a present to the Lord Mayor of thirty guineas in connection with the grant of a Livery occasioned no scandal.

When the Aldermen made their report on the status of the Livery in 1694, there were 700 coaches in London. The last of the sedan chairs disappeared from the streets in 1678.

4 Court and Officers

THE Coachmakers' and Coach Harness Makers' Company of London had, from the beginning, a strong membership. Actual numbers when King Charles II granted the Charter in 1677 are unknown, but an indication was provided ten years later. Richard Cheslyn, the Clerk, opened a new Minute Book in 1687. With enthusiasm still fresh – he had not long been appointed – he started to fill the first pages with the names, in alphabetical order, of all the coachmakers. At S the list stopped and the six pages following were left blank and never penned. But to S – Stephenson – there were 386 names.

Charter troubles happily disposed of, but at a cost which made the Company penurious for years, the ruling body got to work. For the first 25 years of incorporation the Coachmakers did not possess a Hall. The Court usually met in Painter-Stainers' Hall by Queenhithe, then newly-built after the Great Fire of London had destroyed most of the City within the walls. Thoughts of staying may have arisen, for permission was asked to hang the Company's arms in the parlour. However, this use (at £10 per annum rental) lasted only for eight years, till 1686.

Thereafter, till the purchase and refitting of the Company's own Hall in 1703, the Court of Assistants is most often found assembled in the Jewell Chamber at Guildhall, and on occasion did its business in taverns.

Master, three Wardens – senior, renter and junior – and 23 Assistants today constitute the Court, as provided by King Charles II's charter. In all respects the constitution and working of the Company is in accordance with the charter, save that certain powers have, in the passage of time, become obsolete. The fellowship is broad based, good conduct being the substantial qualification. A candidate for admission must be introduced by an Assistant, after due notice has been given. Freedom may be obtained by patrimony, servitude or redemption. The usual practice is to choose the Master and Wardens by rotation.

35

On this last point, a dispute arose in the Company's early years. An appeal was made to the Court of Aldermen which, after weighty consideration, on the 6th March 1678 ordered that the Master and Wardens "should be elected by seniority, unless there be good and sufficient cause to pass over the person next in course."

Appendix B is a complete list of Masters and Clerks of the Company since the foundation. It has been checked from the records, and may be accepted as more accurate than previous lists.

The Renter Warden did not obtain that title until 1697; originally he was "Second Warden". He received all monies and also had charge of all the Company's assets, so was required to find guarantors on admission to office. A Mr. Henry Girle was chosen and, on refusing to serve, was fined £10 . . . .

> . . . . but he alleiging how unfitt he was to performe the said office by reason he could neither write nor read, the Company mitigated the fine to £5.

The Charter, after naming the first Master, Wardens and Assistants, arranges for their replacement as necessary, and comes to the appointment of "one honest and discreet person" as Clerk; to him alone are these epithets applied, which is perhaps a tribute to the responsibility the Clerk always carries. George Daggett was appointed Clerk shortly after the incorporation and was duly sworn to hold office during the pleasure of the Company. His salary was fixed, none too liberally, at £8 a year, but in addition he took a small fee at the registration of each apprentice. It was not until 1765 that the emoluments of office were raised to £43 per annum. That was thought too much soon after, and the unfortunate Clerk of 1787 (Mr. Collingridge) had the dismal experience of writing out the following Order, and on Election Day!

> *1 Sept. 1787.* The Court having taken the salary which is at present paid to the Clerk of the Company into their consideration, and having thought that the same is more than adequate to the trouble of the office, therefore it is Ordered that the Salary hereafter to be paid to the said Clerk shall be at and after the rate of

twenty guineas per annum, and that the same shall continue at that rate so long as the Court shall think fit.

Like the Clerk, the Beadle figures in the Charter. "John the Beadle," whom we first meet, was John Phelps and his salary was £5 a year, but he, too, took certain small fees and he was admitted to the freedom of the Company. When the Company came to own its Hall, it was the Clerk who was given quarters there. But the Court of Assistants, careful of its finances, decided that in consideration of free lodging the Clerk must lower his salary – the salary still being the same £8 a year. The Beadle had lodging found near by without abatement of his salary.

Later the practise varied, sometimes the Clerk, sometimes the Beadle and on occasion of a non-residential beadle, a deputy occupied snug housing at the Hall. A page of the Order Books contains this sententious observation:

> *13 July 1786.* It being reported that Mr. Thos. Parkinson their late beadle was dead it is the opinion of the Gentlemen present that the office of Beadle is vacant.

One class of officers has disappeared, the Stewards. They were the most unfortunate of all. They were chosen by the Court; any person elected Steward and refusing to serve had to forfeit £15. Their sole duty, so far as it is on record, was to provide, at their own expense, breakfast or dinner for the Court and Livery when assembled to honour Lord Mayor's Day. The forfeits brought in a revenue which was not to be despised.

The office was, however, a stepping stone to the Court. The Ordinances state that no person shall be elected Assistant unless he has served as Steward or paid the Steward's forfeit. The records of a neighbourly City Company, the Wheelwrights, state that Stewards were chosen "for the preservation of amity and brotherly love in this Society", though how that end was served by their creation as hosts willy-nilly was perhaps more apparent three centuries ago than it is today.

Mention of the office of Steward in the Ordinances and its occurrence in other City Companies, makes plain that it was an ancient survival. But the election of Stewards gave constant

PLATE 4
William Roberts, the Beadle of the Coachmakers' Company 1892–1904. The mace, still in use, dates from the time of Charles II.

trouble. In 1687 an order had to be made by the Court of Aldermen that the Stewards of the Coachmakers' Company should perform their duty "as becomes good citizens and according to the oath taken to the said Company."

Later we hear of three such officers, "having been elected and chosen Stewards for providing a dinner for the Master and War-dens, Assistants and Livery of this Company on Lord Mayor's Day next ensuing, they had utterly refused to take such office upon them." The Court directed that the protestors should be sum-moned before the Lord Mayor for their contempt. But coercion failed to achieve its purpose. After a time it was found impossible to get the office filled. Long ago it fell into disuse, the charge for entertainment being borne by the general fund. In practice, the certain fee or fine which today is payable on admission to the Court has taken the place of the uncertain cost of providing the dinner.

The original Ordinances have been but slightly varied in three centuries and, in the main, they now govern the management of the Company.

The Coachmakers, once they were in a position to enjoy incorporation, had their responsibilities brought home. In 1690 the Queen – William III's Consort, Mary – required £200,000 from the City by way of a loan for the speedy setting out of the Fleets. The Company lent £200, which was repaid and lent again "for their Majesties' service in Ireland" – and lent again. By December 1696 the demands became imperative: stock (capital) and voluntary subscription, all were needed:

> The Master having received a precept from the Lord Mayor recitcing that his Majesty haveing great occasion for money had by ye Lord Keeper and others desired the City to advance some, and that the City had promised to use their endeavours, & requiring ye Master to sumon the Company together to lend what money they had in stock and to procure what subscrip-tions they could from their members for more. The Court being now sumon'd to the said precept the same was read, And there being no mony of the Company's in the Warden's hands the Master proposed a sub-scription . . . .

For the subscription, three members of the Company put up £20 each, two others £10 and four more £5 each, making the respectable total of £100.

From the Lord Mayor on the 18th October 1697 came a

precept to be "in readiness to receive the King at his coming into England" after the Peace of Ryswick. With King James II's shabby treatment of the Company in mind, the Coachmakers loyally turned out to greet King William as he passed St. Paul's. There was at the same time the Lord Mayor's precept to advance money by way of loan for the King's wants. But the Company had none of that and frankly said so. Its best effort was a subscription by seven members, which produced £90.

Yet in 1701 the Coachmakers were able to contribute £200 towards the City's new loan to the Government. Happily the institution of the Bank of England in King William III's reign and its successful working put an end to the system of extorting such "voluntary" loans. The Bank lent money with the authority of Parliament.

But the Company still had its troubles – major and minor. There was rebellion among journeymen in the trade. Several of them were reported to the Court in the year 1700 for being refractory and disobedient to the orders of the Company and having neglected to pay their quarterage. It was ordered that no member should employ them on pain of 5s. fine for every day of such employment – a very severe penalty. Certain journeymen who did not keep a public shop employed other journeymen, thereby creating disorder and confusion and evasion of the laws of the Company for searching out ill-made goods. This was put down by a penalty not exceeding £5. Other men, "foreigners", followed the coachmaker's trade unlawfully. These were prosecuted.

In 1721 the Coachmakers' workmen were stigmatised for having entered into combination to raise wages, thereby setting "a very ill example to journeymen in all other trades."

The old guild organisations included both masters and men within the fold, but their democratic tendencies have been much exaggerated. Of necessity the master class ruled, when few indeed of the workmen could read and write and cast accounts. A disturbance of unusual gravity occurred on a Lord Mayor's Day, when the Coachmakers' and Coach Harness Makers' Company was accustomed to hold its great feast in Hall on the return of the Court of Assistants and Liverymen from attendance on the Lord Mayor.

The Clerk's brief record runs as follows:

19 Nov. 1724. In the affair relating to the Riott comit-
ted by severall journemen and others at the Hall on the
last Lord Mayor's day, it was ordered that the prosecu-
con should be in the Kings Bench, if proper. The Renter
Warden should pay the Chirurgeon his demands for
attending the watchman who was wounded in the riott,
and since dyed, and the Warden give some reasonable
releife to the poor widdow.

It was a minor upset which agitated the Company when the
Master of 1698, Thomas Kirkham, found himself in heated
controversy with the Court. It arose over a certain "blew cloth"
which the Company proudly displayed on its stand at the greeting
to King William already alluded to. Order had been given that
this cloth should not be embroidered, yet the Master had had
this done, at a charge of £15 8s. 6d. to the Company's funds. In
this nefarious act he had the agreement – in writing – of several
members of the Company. The argument had a somewhat lame
conclusion:

> It is this day declared by this Court that the taking of
> such subscription was a misdemeanour in the Master,
> and contrary to the constitution of the Company. And
> that it is not in the power of any Master or Wardens of
> the Company to expend or lay out any sums of the
> Company's mony exceeding forty shillings without the
> consent of this Court unless in ye ordinary charge of
> the Company. And therefore the said Mr. Kirkham is
> fined one shilling for the said misdemeanour.

Master Kirkham's vanity apparently had added to his offence.
He had put his own initials on the stand's "blew cloth." They
were ordered to be taken out and the Queen's cypher placed
thereon instead.

The Company has no charitable foundations. It told the Livery
Companies' Commission of 1884 that it had never had any
property given, devised or bequeathed to it since the time of the
charter onward.

But the Coachmakers' and Coach Harness Makers' Company
throughout its long history has supported, and supports today, all

trade charities; it has granted donations and sometimes pensions. Its aid given to technical education in the trade and given enthusiastically, must await mention till later pages; in the days of Queen Anne and the Four Georges apprenticeship prevailed and the workshop was the only school. Night-classes, poly-technics, technical education – how such new-fangled ideas would have puzzled our ancestors, who themselves learnt all they knew in the shop!

Charity is universal. Its operation might even extend to a Master. In 1760 Mr. John Virgoe was Master. Four years later John Virgoe is reported to be chosen as Beadle. He must have fallen on evil days.

This did occasionally happen to a Master:

> *28 Apr. 1768.* Mr. John Westley, the late Master of this Company, being represented to this Court to be in distressed circumstances, Ordered that the said John Westley be allowed out of the Company's estate, the sum of £12 per annum, to be paid him quarterly by the Renter Warden for the time being (till further Order) at Midsumer, Michas, Xmas, and Ladyday, and that one quarter's payment be imediately made him in advance and another on Midsumer day next.

The very beautiful Poor Box of 1680 was passed round for collections and its good use must have brought blessings upon the Company.

The following cases are taken out of many:

> *13 Mar. 1788.* Mrs. Mary Preston, the widow of one of the late members of this Company, having presented a petition to this Court stating her age and infirmities & that she was greatly distressed in point of circumstances, & thereby praying relief . . . .

it was ordered that she be paid a guinea by the Renter Warden, who was further directed "to admit her on the list of the poor." The meaning of this last phrase appears in a similar case, that of Mary Lloyd:

1 Sep. 1789. The Court, on taking such petition into consideration & being informed that there was a vacancy in the poor widows' list (the number of which amounts to 8), by the death of Mrs. Wrench ordered Mary Lloyd to attend next Court to receive the usual bene-faction.

These widows received four shillings a month each; their number never seemed to exceed nine, but might sink to seven.

5 Apprentices and Freemen

APPRENTICES in the coachbuilding and coach harness making trades had to be bound in the presence of the Court, at times represented by certain Assistants and the Clerk, who kept a register. The rules governing the taking of apprentices and restricting their number were rigidly observed. Transgressors became a constant source of trouble:

> *15 Oct. 1678*. Ordered that Mr. Parsons be fined for takeing an Apprentice above his number, and not binding him at the Company, nor before the Master nor Wardens, nor by the Clerke, contrary to the Ordinances whereunto he is sworne.

> *5 Aug. 1679*. Mr. Crawley came this day to bind an Apprentice it appeared, and he said and confess'd that he had an Apprentice whose tearme is not yet expired, whoe is run away and is a Souldier and a theife to him, and that he would never accept him for his servant. And further confessed and promised that George Parrish, his brother in Law that lived with him, he would not teach nor instruct, nor cause to be taught nor instructed in the said trade while he lives with him, and that he would pay all the forfeitures by the Ordinances which he forfeites thereby, all which he promised to performe and not to accept of the said Apprentice nor instruct his said Kinsman and hath sett his hand hereunto.
>
> [Signed] THOS. CRAWLEY.

On the whole one gathers that the interests of the apprentice were really guarded by the Court:

> *30 June 1709*. Wm. Wright, who was bound to Jacob Smith for Edward Wootton, complaining against his Master for hard usage and his Master not having

taken his Freedom of ye City, desired to be turned over to Mr. Phillips.

The case came up on 11th August when Mr. Wootton "complained much of his apprentice" but Wright retorted that he "had not victuals nor work" and it was ordered that he might be turned over* to another master.

Without definite evidence of service the Court was reluctant to give admission to the Company; the first instance on record is that of a man whose case was allowed:

> *10 Sep. 1679.* Mr. John Johnson appeared this day and, upon hearing what he could say himselfe and also the evidence that Mr. Robt. Johnson gave on his behalfe, it appeared he was bound to the Trade and his Master breaking he was afterwards turn'd over to his brother, and that he served him in that time and after his Indenture was out above seaven years, and lived with him and in his family and had meat, drink, lodging, and washing for above 7 yeares, and followed and used that trade, and he gave him wages, but it was out of kindness to him as a Brother, and that he was bound to this Trade and never followed or learned any other, nor hath no other way to live on but by this trade . . . .

The Court finally accepted Mr. John Johnson as a member of the Company upon his giving a bond for £20 "for the use of the Company on or before the next Lord Mayor's Day" and a gratuity towards the charges . . . . "whereupon Mr. Johnson gave bond and tooke his Oath accordingly."

In early days there was occasional conflict between the Coachmakers' Company and older Companies whose members it had taken in:

> *1 April 1679.* It is on voate by the generall consent of the Court of Assistants ordered this day that all persons free of this Company shall, upon their complaint to this Company, be defended at the Company's charge against all suits & troubles that shalbe brought against them about any claime due, or demand that shalbe by any

*The phrase "turn over" or "turn to" expresses the transfer of indentures to someone able to accept an apprentice. If a master died during the term prescribed by the indentures, the apprentice was turned over to another master; such a transfer had to be approved by the Court.

other Company whereof they were before free,—save
only for Quarteridge.

8 July 1679. All apprentices made free of this Company that were bound to other Companys be indempni-
fyed and saved harmless from all suits by workeing in
London, at the charge of this Company; and that the
Wardens disburse and pay the same.

Amongst the papers at Guildhall* is the humble petition of
William Fuller, read on 2nd March 1708. He says that he was
made free in the Company of Leathersellers about the year
1675, though brought up as a coachmaker; he then goes on to
inform the Court of Aldermen:

> Your Petitioner has bin set up in the said trade about
> 7 years past, and when the Coachmakers obtained their
> Charter of Incorporation they persuaded your Peti-
> tioner, being ignorant of the Customes of this City, to
> subscribe a writing whereby he obliged himselfe to
> conform to the By Laws of that Company, pretending
> that they would save him harmless from any expence he
> should be put unto by reason of his being free of the
> Leathersellers. Your petitioner having subscribed such
> writing the Coachmakers have compelled him to serve
> the offices of usher and steward in that Company, and
> threaten to sue him unless he becomes Free of them, for
> which he is to pay a fine, besides a further sume if he
> should be called to take their Livery upon him.
> The Company of Leathersellers, whereof your
> petitioner is free, are likewise pressing that he should
> take their Cloathing, by means of which several Com-
> panys your petitioner is like to be put to great expences,
> and he having sustained great losses in trade—the same
> may be his utter undoing unless timely relieved by the
> aid of this Hono^ble Court.

How far this was genuine it is difficult to say in view of the
Coachmakers' reply embodied in a lengthy minute. The part
dealing directly with the petition is as follows:

*Guildhall Miscellaneous Docu-
ments: Companies, 2–2.

1 Apr. 1708. The Petitioner voluntarily came in and subscribed and swore as above, the Coachmakers never gave him any promise to save him harmless from the Leather Sellers. The suggestion in the Petition yt the Coy. of Coachmakers threaten to sue the petitioner unless he becomes free of them, for which he is to pay twenty pounds, is utterly false & ridiculous for he is already free for which he only paid a Guinea, and the Coachmakers demand nothing of him but two shillings p.a. Quarterage. The Coy. of Coachmakers humbly conceive, by virtue of certain orders of this Court settling the qualification of persons compelled to take yᵉ Cloathing or Livery,—the petitioner is very safe from that charge, & in no danger of being called upon by either Company to take yᵉ Office upon him.

The last sentence suggests that in the view of the Coachmakers' Court, Mr. Fuller was never likely to advance beyond the humble station in which he then found himself.

A remarkable practise in connection with apprenticeship occurs in the early days of the Company, when a large number of apprentices were bound to William Watson, and immediately "turned over" to someone else.* It necessarily followed that Assistants and senior members of the Coachmakers' Company for many years after its incorporation were men who had served their apprenticeship with other Companies and had taken their freedom. They now found the charges and responsibilities of membership of two Companies burdensome. In order to ensure a supply of new apprentices, and at the same time to avoid their being subject to the double liability, the Coachmakers' Company hit on the expedient of making Watson a freeman by redemption. He was, as a Committee at Guildhall described him, "a nominal person" appointed to bind apprentices with the intention that they might be turned over to freemen of kindred trades, though not of the Coachmakers' Company, becoming freemen Coachmakers when their apprenticeship expired.

Watson died before several of those so bound to him were out of their indentures, when others had completed apprenticeship but had not taken up the freedom, and yet others through negligence had not been turned over. The Chamberlain of

*Guildhall Miscellaneous Documents: Companies, 6–14.

London refused to receive these apprentices and ex-apprentices at loose ends as freemen Coachmakers by servitude. Guildhall could do nothing better than suggest to the Coachmakers' Company that it should admit them into the freedom by redemption, in the circumstances taking only a very small fine.

An attempt was made in 1700 and 1701 to get Mr. Jacob Smith (presumably he who had been Master in 1691) to play the part of "nominal person" which Mr. Watson had played, but this had a short life. The tangled business of nominal apprenticeship with the avowed intention of turning over to another Company became unnecessary when the Coachmakers themselves were sufficiently numerous and organised to carry all their own apprentices.

In the middle 18th-century there was a movement to allow each member to take an additional apprentice and for a time this was conceded. Ultimately, in 1762, the number of apprentices permissible was raised to four.

The earlier apprentices were largely drawn from the ranks of husbandmen, farmers and yeomen; but in the 18th-century, when the coachmaking business was rising to its height, many more were sons of tradesmen, particularly "victuallers", innkeepers and others associated with the movement of traffic on the roads.

Not infrequently, for the binding of apprentices, members of the Court and the Clerk met at various taverns. Lists of the old London hostelries, now mostly forgotten, which served this use are printed in Appendix E.

The consideration money for the indentures varied very greatly, from £10 to £80 in 1765; perhaps about £30 would be a fair average sum. There were cases of the son of a deceased member receiving indentures for nothing, and still more of an apparent uncle coachmaker in London making no charge for his nephew from the provinces. Several times the consideration money for binding was supplemented by a grant from Christ's Hospital, the Society for Distressed Clergy and local charities. At the end of the 18th-century apprentices were few and premiums were seldom obtained, but just before they expired a certain coachmaker named John Browne, who lived on Fish Street Hill, secured a premium of £200 from a Worcester wine merchant; this was in 1787. Mr. Browne, fired by this success, extracted £500 from a brewer of Limehouse in 1791 and his final effort in the same year squeezed 500 guineas from a Herefordshire "esquire." That was five times as much as anybody else ever had and, possibly to appease his conscience, Mr. Browne afterwards took Henry Trollop, "late one of the boys of the Foundling Hospital", for nothing.

6 Matters of Discipline

AMONG the many matters which occupied the attention of the Court of Assistants in the early years of the Company was that of maintaining order in the trade. There were always delinquents waiting to drive a breach through the rules once a vigilant watch was relaxed:

> *2 Oct. 1701.* That the Master & Wardens take care to convict and prosecute the men at Colebrook, Sheene, & Kingston, and all others that follow the Trade unlawfully within the Precincts of the Charter, & take such assistance & use such methods as they shall be advised is necessary.

> *1 Oct. 1702.* Mr. Short appeared upon sumons for imploying a Forreigner was, upon submission to the Court, fined 20ˢ· & paid the same.
> Mr. Talbott sumoned for the same offence & not appearing was fined.

> *29 Mar. 1706.* Mr. Kitson be sumoned to next Court for imploying a Shoemaker, he having not appear'd after 3 Summonses is fined 3ˢ· 4ᵈ· per time.

> *9 Aug. 1716.* John Ironmonger appeared and was acquainted with his offence committed in keeping a fforreigner at work in the Trade, he seemed to justify himself and departed in contempt of the Court.

Biding its time, the Court six months later fined John Ironmonger £10; that was after discovering that he still kept the "foreigner" employed despite a promise given to get rid of him.

> *13 Jan. 1698.* A wheeler at Hackney was summon'd for putting in a Pearch, he appeared and submitted to the

Court & promised to doe soe no more, and was thereupon discharged.

A perch was the centre pole connecting the fore and hind axles
of a coach – a very vital timber.

> *2 Dec. 1708.* Robt Nash informed the Court that
> John Law, of Bow, C^o. Middlesex, wheelwright, put in
> 2 axle trees & a Riding Bed for Mr. Culliford, a Gent.
> living near there,—Nash to bring evidence against Law.

> *5 July 1734.* Matthew Bateman, a wheeler and free-
> man of London, useth and exerciseth the trades of a
> coachmaker and coachharnessmaker in the parish of
> S^t. Mary Whitechapple, als Matfellon, for his own
> proffit and benefit, not being lawfully intituled so to do.
> In support it was alledged that the said Matthew Bate-
> man about June last undertook, and did make, sell, and
> deliver a new Chariot with a Carriage and pair of
> Harness for and to Mr. John Hyde, merchant, in Rood
> Lane, London, of the value of £30 or thereabouts, &
> that the delivery thereof was within the City of London.
> That Robert Preston (also apprehended no freeman
> of the City or Company), trimmed the body and cut out
> the harness, and that King, a wheeler by trade, and no
> freeman, made the body.
> That Matt. Bateman about a year since made a
> machine chariot for Mr. March of Austin Fryars,
> London, merchant, of the value of £70, which it is
> apprehended was made by the same hands.
> That about the same time he made a Machine Chariot
> for George Griffin Esquire, of Plaistow in Essex about
> four miles from London, of the value of £40 . . . . also
> made by the same hands.

A case was drawn up against Matthew Bateman and it was to
be referred to the Common Serjeant for his opinion; perhaps that
was adverse to a prosecution, because no more is heard of it.

On 13th August 1752 William Beech and John Orme were
"unanimously fined £5 each for imploying forreigners." At the

same time the question was raised as to reviewing by-laws "which restrein the Number of Apprentices, concerning Forreigners working at the Trades, and relating to Masters employing Forreigners." This started a case which dragged on for some years. A long minute, hopelessly confused, indicates some of the difficulties in the way:

> *23 Nov. 1752.* The Master reported that he & the Wardens having had a long consultacon with the council [counsel] relating to the affair with Mr. Beech and Mr. Orme,—the Councell were unanimously of opinion that the Company's By-Law was very unintelligible, & Ill-penned, but that at present they agreed it was inadvisable to hazard a Tryal before they made a new By-Law, yet not to go on to Tryal till a proper Comittee had duely taken fully and clearly all the proofs relating to those affairs they cou'd possibly get, distinguishing which evidence were free and which were not free of the Company, and which had been apprentice to the Trades and which not, and how and in what manner in particular the Forreigners employ'd were taught and instructed in the Trades, and by whom and in what manner they were employ'd, and that then they wou'd, if the Company thought proper, give their more full thoughts upon the affair.

After six years, Mr. Beech's affair still caused disquiet. The Clerk asked whether he was to proceed further, and was ordered to do so; but apparently the whole matter was allowed to drop. Later Mr. Beech paid a £10 fine "for not serving ye office of an Assistant."

The search conducted by the Company under its charter powers fulfilled a double purpose. It was a most effective disciplinary weapon for ensuring obedience, and at the same time it gave protection to the public against fraudulent workmanship which only the expert eye could detect. The town was divided into four "Walks", their original names being Outwalk, Piccadilly Walk, Middle Walk, and Cow Lane Walk. A Warden, or the Master of the year, was always with the party, representing authority, with three or four others. Apparently they made a long day's work of it, for orders survive for assemblies at six o'clock on a summer's morning. That there was good hunting on these occasions is made clear by the following list of coachmakers and coach harness makers, found in default after a search on the 5th April 1678:

Mr. Ironmonger	..	old ironworke
Mr. Atkinson	..	old curbs—excused
Mr. Bentley ..	..	old stuffing & hay
Mr. Onion ..	..	old iron & foot-board stays
Mr. Parratt ..	..	old pearch & old iron
Mr. Lindsey	..	Hay, old standards, old iron, & a pearch
Mr. Gawthropp	..	Hay, old iron fircholds,* old roof railes
Mr. Kempe ..	..	Forewarned
Mr. Rowett ..	..	all old iron
Richd Shorter	..	old Timber in ye roofe, old Iron, old curbs
John Johnson	..	Old iron in new Coach
Wm. Clerke ..	..	Old Bootes, old iron in 2 Coaches
Mr. Purse ..	..	old Iron, a paire old curbs
Mr. Carey ..	..	Traces lined with Basill
Mr. Cheshire Mr. Anderson	..	Old Basill & old polepeece

On the last day of April 1678, Mr. Hooper was fined 40s. for refusing to be searched and Messrs. Carey and Rog. Taylor were fined 2s. 6d. each for "ill wares."

An order of 19th March 1680 refers to the coach of no less a person than the Earl of Danby, afterwards Duke of Leeds:

Mr. Hooper on search for haveing old iron on 2 Coaches, the Lord Trear Coach all old iron & old timber in the body, another coach old Tongue and plate; upon voate and order of the Company this day he is fined by this Court Seaven pounds for his ill and irregular, and not good wares and worke, which fine is ordered to be demanded according to Law, and in default of payment

*This word should be "futchells". Part of the fore-carriage of a four-wheeler with a "pole" to which the two-wheeler horses are harnessed. There are two futchells, mounted on the pivot point and running forward. They are usually carved; they run parallel with a gap between them into which the pole nests at its rear end. The pole is effectively the tiller to the forecarriage.

53

to be prosecuted at Law for the same unless he can next Court shew good cause to the contrary.

On the same day:

> Mr. Robert Johnson fined for putting Red Basill sheepskins in the back of a new coach, and noe other leather, nor neath* Leather, by order of Court 20ˢ·

—afterwards reduced to 5s.

> Mr. Nevill, on a voate by this Court, was fined 40ˢ· for imploying a Dutchman, not free nor admitted of this Compy, and for shewing and teaching him the Art & trade contrary to the Ordinances. Mr. Nevill, on voate this day, was fined for putting in Basill and sheepskins for welting of 20 houseinges or more. Probatum per Mr. Rose, yᵉ Coppersmith that shidded them.

However, Mr. Nevill, after due consideration, "referred him-selfe" to the Court and both fines were remitted to 10s. cash down.

In June 1679 it was ordered that . . . .

> . . . . Mr. Awbry be sumoned to be at next Court, to shew cause why he should not be fined for putting an old Carriage to the Queen's body Coach, and to ask him how long he hath been a Trader for himselfe.

On 8th July, however, Mr. Awbry was "discharged from any fine because the old body was put in by the Duke of Monmouth and Sir William Armestrong." The Duke was probably thinking of other matters, as he was banished within two months of this date.

What relation Mr. Awbry was to Samuel (the donor of the cup) is not clear, but he evidently had a good business, as will be seen from the following references to him amidst a batch of offenders:

> *9 Oct. 1679.* A carriage at Mr. Polehamptons—rotten cross-barrs, old pearch, knotty standards, & 2 old plates

*Leather from neat cattle – of the ox or cow kind, while basil is made only from sheep.

54

belonging to Mr. Obediah Bentley; on voate fined for the same 40^s.

Mr. Awbery for old Standards and old Ironworke in the Dutches of Southampton's Coach, it being a rich one, whereby he saves, and also for imploying Mr. Rawliston, not being free of this Company. On voate was fined for ye same.

Mr. Ironmonger a small new Charriott, the hind windowes & sides calves skin, the back and boote old leather.—On voate fined for the same.

The whole business of the search must have been most unpleasant, and it is not surprising to find that members sometimes refused to carry out their duties:

17 Nov. 1696. Mr. Robt. Carter finded for not going 3 searches, nor appearing on Lord Mayor's Day, & being now present was desired to pay the Fines, or leave himselfe to the Courte & they might moderate the fines, but he was refractory & refused so to doe, whereupon & after frequent admonitions it was ordered that he be sumoned before the Lord Mayor.

4 Dec. 1696. Mr. Carter, being sumoned before the Lord Mayor, appeared & upon opening the matter & informing my Lord how many defaults he had made, & how fairly the Company had offered him if he would leave himselfe to them, My Lord Mayor told him he did very ill in giving the Company trouble, & that he ought to submitt himselfe to his Company & in case he did not the Court of Aldermen would compell them. Whereupon he desired it might be left to my Lord to moderate his fines, & promised to observe the Company's sumons for the future, which the Company readily complied with, and thereupon my Lord Mayor ordered him to pay 25^s. for the fines, & the clerke & Beadle's fees on his swearing on ye Livery.

Then on 28th March 1701 the following order was made:

> All members that have served as Master of this Company be excused from going on Searches, and all other members that have not yet served as Masters shall, from time to time after they shall have served as Masters, be excused from going on Searches. One Assistant with yᵉ Master or a Warden and a Liveryman shall be sufficient on any search.

By 1757 there was obviously the intention of dropping the search altogether, and it was suspended until the Court should think fit to order the contrary. Though faults in coachbuilding mostly caught the keen eyes of the searchers, complaints relating to harness also occurred, and therein was a risk of clashing with the older Company, the Saddlers, who obtained their Charter from King James I in 1605. By the courtesy of the Clerk of the Saddlers' Company, it is possible to give an extract from the minutes of their Quarter Court, held on 18th October, 1704:

> Ordered that the Court do acquaint Mr. Jacob, clerk of the Coachmakers' Company, with the Act of Parliament empowering this Company to search the Coachmakers and oblidge them to pay Quarteridge, and to give them a copy of the Attorney-Generall's opinion thereon, and to desire a speedy answer from the Coachmakers touching the same.

Not hurring, the Coachmakers considered the matter for five months, then wrote as follows to Mr. Draper, the clerk of the Saddlers' Company, on 20th April 1705:

> I communicated the Case you left with me to the Company of Coachmakers at a full Court, and read to them the Act of Parliament and all the answer they made was: That that statute was made for a limited time & they believe it is not continued, & hope it is not. That they doe not think it necessary to trouble Councell to consider whether the Letter of yᵗ Act subjects them to search of your Company, but are well satisfyed they are not within yᵉ equity & meaning of it as their case now stands.

That the Coachmakers have been many years a distinct Corporacon and have power of searching their own members and take great care in doing it so as to prevent all abuses.

That they doe not desire any difference with the Company of Sadlers, but can by noe means consent to come under the search or Government of another Corporation.

This is all the answer I have to return, who am

Yo^r very humble serv^t.

JOHN JACOB.

As was usual with the Livery Companies, great difficulty was experienced in collecting the "quarterage" or subscription of members, which was originally only 2s. per annum. The trouble of collection caused arrears to accumulate at all times. Sometimes the employer came to the rescue by paying the workman's dues himself. In practise it often appears that the masters paid only when they wished to register a new apprentice; this gave the Company some hold upon them; and the journeymen paid only when the masters exerted pressure, and if they were themselves defaulters they probably did little.

As regards discipline generally within the Company, the Court was insistent that due order be maintained:

16th April 1678. Mr. Rix appeared this day and to be sumoned next Court to answer Mr. Warden Phillipps' complaint for his ill words and usage and sinister means to obteyene his custom.

30 Mar. 1704. Mr. John Golding appear'd upon sumons for abusing the Beadle & upon his submission & promise not to offend again was excused. Mrs. Atkins, being sumoned for using old Iron & giving abusive Language to the beadle, upon her promise not to doe the like for the future was excused.

10 May 1705. Mr. Thos. Burge summoned to appear for not attending on Thanksgiving Day was fined 3s. 4d., which he refused to pay.

[Mr. Allatt alike summoned and fined.]

That Mr. Thomas Burge and Mr. Allatt be summoned to appear before the Lord Mayor on Tuesday next at 8 o'clock to answer for their contempt of this Court.

Against this may be set two examples of the Court's benevolence:

30 June 1698. Mr. Rich^d. Strutton, a Livery man of this Company, have given him, he being in great want in prison, and that his voluntary surrender of ye Clothing of this Company be accepted.

30 Sep. 1703. That Tho. Rowett having served in the Wars be made free.

In a bundle of old legal papers at the Hall there was a very complete *dossier* of a case which failed in itself, but contained some particulars of considerable interest. The action would never have been started if Mr. John Tovey, the faithful Clerk for many years and donor of the two-handled cup in 1718 when he was first appointed, had been trusted; for he was asked to reply to three questions, one of them being whether the Company could sue a foreigner who worked at the trade with any prospect of success. His answer, dated 30th June, 1752, and addressed to the Master, Daniel Cogdell, was generally in the affirmative but with this proviso . . . .

. . . . under a supposition that the facts can and will be fully and fairly proved, and also that he be not a wheeler, for in that case (as I ever did) I think it hazardous to venture a Tryal.

In spite of this the Company decided in 1754 to have a test case with a "wheeler", or wheelwright. They found one against whom they charged offences ranging over 11 months; on six counts penalties totalling £132 were claimed.

The Company's "person whose name is made use of on this occasion" was Mr. John Smith, whose undistinguished patronymic made the defendant doubt whether he really existed; he did and was a perfectly good coachmaker, free of the Company, who plied his trade in Little Queen Street, Lincoln's Inn Fields. The defendant was Mr. John Miles, who lived in Camomile Street. His story is best told from the brief drawn up for counsel:

> He was bred a Wheelwright and serv'd his time to that trade only, and for several years last past hath confined himself to the exercise of that Business only, and has thereby acquired a very considerable Fortune, and was in as extensive Business as any Wheelwright in London. But being a very avaritious Person and one who cares not how little his Neighbour gets so that he can but get an Advantage to himself, he about a year ago took it into his Head to set up the Trade of a Coach maker and Coach Harness maker, and to follow that Trade as well as the Trade of a wheelwright, and without any the least Knowledge in the trade of coach making, he undertook to do all sorts of that business for his own Lucre and Benefit, and employed some journeymen coach makers and wheelers for the doing thereof, and as Mr. Miles was a wheeler and was one who was employed as well by Gentlemen to make their wheels as also by the Coach makers, he had frequent opportunities of recommending himself to Jobbs, sometimes in new work, but more principally in repairing coaches and coach harness, and for the space of about a year last past he has been considerably employed both in the Coachmaking and harness making way, and refuses to Decline the same although all persuasive Methods have been tried to bring him thereto without effect.

The action was based upon that part of the Charter which provided that none save those who were free of the Company should exercise the "trades, arts, or misteries of a coach maker .... upon such pains, penalties and punishments as by the Laws and Statutes of this realm can or may be lawfully inflicted." The reference here was to the Act 5 Elizabeth, ch. 31 (1563), and the difficulty was to prove that the Act took cognisance of coaches, when the word itself was barely known and, possibly, none were being made in England. To get over this difficulty the lawyers

PLATE 5
A Coachmaker.

cited Letters Patent of Queen Mary, dated 29th May 1554, which tell how:

> We of our specyall Grace, certayne knowledge, and mere mocyon have named, made, and appoynted our welbylovyd servaunt Anthony Silver to have the rowme

PLATE 6
A Wheelwright.

or offyce of maker of all our close carres, charetts, and waggons . . . . And we of our grace especyall aforesayd do gyve and graunt by these presents . . . . to the sayd Anthony Silver for his Lyverye Cote incydent to hym for his sayd office three yards of redde clothe of tenne Shillyngs the yarde, two yards of blacke velvett to

garde the same cote, and syx yards of fryse for the
lyninge thereof, with the makynge and embroderynge
of the letters M and R. The same to be hade, and yerely
perceyved to the sayd Anthonye Silver durynge his sayd
lyf by the handes of the Master of our grete Warderob
for the tyme beinge.

"Carres, charetts and waggons" may be understood by the
average person as comprising coaches, but it strains law to make
an Act of Parliament imposing penalties apply to a trade which in
its time might be said to be non-existent – unborn. Rather weakly
seeking to cover its retreat by a declaration that can have con-
vinced nobody, the Company decided not to proceed to trial and
reluctantly paid the defendant's costs.

Over 30 years later another action was mooted. This was in
1789, when Charles Barker, a freeman of the Company since 4th
December 1788, had taken as partner William Runciman, who
had never been apprenticed, and the proposed action was to be
against Barker for infringement of the by-laws. This, too, was not
pursued; the law at that date did not regard with favour too narrow an exercise of the Company's rights.

It is never easy to say with certainty how far the Company was
in funds – or even whether it was immediately solvent; it was not
the custom to distinguish between capital and revenue, nor was
there much occasion in the case of a corporation which had no
profits to distribute, or, for that matter, a limited liability. On
various occasions it was found that liabilities exceeded assets and
all that was needed was a levy upon members – upon such, that is
to say, as were their own masters.

The middle of the 18th-century provided some lean periods,
when Orders such as the following were made:

> *15 Aug. 1758.* In maintenance and support of the
> Justice, Credit, and Reputacon of the Company the
> sum of £275–2–0 would be necessary to be raised,
> contributed, born, and paid in equal proporcons by each
> and every master, Members of the Company, for and
> towards defraying and paying the said necessary charges
> of the Company, and that they had prepared accordingly
> a Charge and Assessment of £2–2–0 on every master a
> member.

This was agreed. In 1776 the excess of liabilities was £400. A little earlier, in 1743, when the liabilities were only £97 2s. 9½d., more than two-thirds arose from debts to:

Mr. Thistleton the vintner	29	5	8
Mr. Savage the cook	39	0	6

In 1739 £100 worth of New South Sea Annuities was bought for £110; in 1743, during a time when the income had failed, this was sold for £119 17s. 6d. with interest. A Minute was made on:

> *21 Mar. 1799.* That the Income of this Company, on the average of three years after reducing such expences as are allowed by the Income Act,—is £153 per annum and that the Clerk be authorized to return the table of Income delivered by the Assessor to him and state that this Co.ʸ is willing to pay on account of such Income £7–13–0 being not less than $\frac{1}{20}$th of such income.

The return was for Pitt's first Income Tax of the year 1799.

Some prospect of civil disorder occasioned the following expenses:

1708
April 10. Paid for a Musket & a collar of bandileers — 15 0
Spent with the Master at buying the Musket — 6
24. Paid the man that goes out upon the Trained Bands — 6 0
Aug. 18. Paid for a yellow knot for the soldier — 6
1709
Mar. 10, 13 & 23. Paid three times to the Trained Bands upon the rising of the mob — 1 19 0

The reference in the last entry relates to the troubles associated with the trial of Dr. Sacheverell.

On 4th January 1769, the Cordwainers' Company was exercised about the necessity for aiding the import of hides and resolved to petition Parliament. A circular letter was sent out to the companies and towns interested in leather, in response to which the Coachmakers' Company subscribed £50. (One-half of this was returned.) Unfortunately for the success of the petition the Tanners did not support it and nothing came of the scheme at that time.

An Act (25 George III, ch. 30) levied a tax upon every shop "publickly kept open for carrying on any trade or for selling any goods wares or merchandize by retail." At the same time it exempted the warehouse "employed solely for the purpose of lodging gods . . . . or carrying on some manufacture."

By another Act passed in the same session (25 George III, c. 49) every coachmaker was required to take out a yearly licence of 20s., and by another section the coachmaker had to pay 20s. for every coach with four wheels, and 10s. for every calash with two wheels, which he should make, build, or construct for sale.

7 Labour and the Cost of Coaches

MODERN complexities of existence require a manufacturer's association and a trade union for organised industry; in the days of the early Georges it was held that so complete was the identity of interests of master and journeymen that they might fittingly be members of the same Company. From the constant difficulty experienced in making the journeyman pay his quarterage, it may be supposed that he felt no assurance that membership meant anything to him after his employment was secured. The Company's records offered only the masters' views about the journeymen. These occurred in 1753, when an increase in the number of apprentices was receiving consideration.

It should be explained, however, that the question first arose many years earlier; there are references to it at Guildhall* in 1718 when very direct encouragement was given by the Court of Aldermen to an increase in the number of apprentices:

> This Court reassuming the consideration of the Complaint against the Master, Wardens, and Assistants of the Company of Coach-makers and Coach harness-makers were of opinion That the By-Law of their Company which prohibits and forbids their members to take above a certain number of apprentices is an unlawful restraint upon the said members in the exercise of their trade, and is the occasion of unjust vexations and prosecutions of the said members, and tends to enhancing the price of their comodities . . . . This Court doth therefore order that the said Master and Wardens do forthwith call together a Court of Assistants of the said Company and repeal the said By-Law.

To vary the important Ordinances which related to apprenticeship required good reasons. What actually is found is a Minute, dated 23rd August 1753, which filled five folio pages in small but exquisite script, and with very few pauses for breath. From all the verbiage some light does emerge upon labour conditions in the

*Guildhall *Repertories*, CXXII, fo. 406; and CXXIII, fo. 10.

craft in the middle 18th-century. The Minute explains why a limit to the number of apprentices working in coachmaking and coach harness making was imposed:

> To preserve a good and proper medium as to the number of apprentices each member of the said Company should have . . . . so that the youth put out to the said trades might, after they had served a laborious apprenticeship, be able to live and support themselves and families as journeymen in a comfortable manner as persons in such a situation of life might, reasonably thinking, expect or deserve without encroaching and imposing upon the masters, members of the said Company, for exorbitant wages (the Bane and Distruction of all Arts, Trades, and Mysteries), to the hurt and prejudice both of the Masters in the said trades and the customers with them dealing.

Orders for coaches by the nobility and gentry had now become numerous. Despite the increase in the numbers of master coachmakers and of journeymen, the latter could not accomplish the work. Why?

> Chiefely and principally because very many or most of the best hands of the Journymen in the said trades— instead of making a just and proper use of the care and indulgence of the said Company towards them by preserving the trades in a good and proper medium for their living and support, have taken a quite contrary course, and by degrees from the time of making the said Orders to this present time have risen to such an intollerable, insufferable, insupportable heighth of self sufficiency and disobedience in behaviour towards the Masters, not in the least submitting to their government, management, or direction,—very many of them refusing to work by the day, or any otherways than by the Great,★ or peice, which is a most grievous and insupportable imposition both on the Masters and Customer.

It was such malcontents who demanded from the master coachmakers . . . .

★"By the great, by great – Of work done; at a fixed price; for the whole amount; by task; by the piece." *Oxford English Dictionary*. It may seem surprising that the employer preferred a day-work rate to a piece-rate, but the coach building trade was not mass production in 1753, nor was it repetition work.

.... unusual and unwarrantable wages,—loosing the time of their said masters by frequent and almost continued Rioting, Drunkenness, and Debauchery,— not only to the hurt and prejudice of themselves and their own families, who ought to and might be comfortably maintained by them, but likewise to the great oppression, hurt, and Damage of their Masters who pay them, and so that it is impossible for the said Masters to get a reasonable support by their business unless they in like manner raise their prices upon their Customers to the certain very great and unreasonable abuse of the Nobility and Gentry of the Nation.

It does seem that the control of labour 200 years ago was not so entirely simple as is sometimes supposed. Whether the journeymen would be much impressed by the plea for the pockets of "the Nobility and Gentry of the Nation" may be open to doubt. There is some evidence that they had their way about piece-work many years later when, on 19th March 1789, a committee was appointed . . . .

.... to consider of some regulation to be made in respect to the prices now paid to the journeymen of this trade, and to draw out a regular set of prices to be paid to the said journeymen by the masters.

After a year, when nothing had been done, the Clerk was ordered to write to Mr. Hatchett requesting him to send an account of prices paid for jobbing-work, both coachmaking and harness making. Mr. John Hatchett had been Master of the Company in 1785, when the *European Magazine* gave an imposing view of his premises in Long Acre with a specimen of his work conspicuous in the foreground. A foreign visitor* in 1786 tells something about the appearance of the interior:

We went to Hatchett, one of London's most famous master saddlers, who employs several hundred workmen in his service. At home we have no conception of such a saddler, with premises for cartwrights, smiths, harness-makers, carvers, painters, upholsterers, gilders, —all kinds of workmen necessary for coach and harness-making, and other accessories, working under his

* *Sophie in London*, published in 1786, a translation from the German of Sophie von La Roche, the friend and correspondent of Goethe.

supervision and producing the loveliest masterpieces of their kind. I cannot think of any visit more interesting than this one; think of three floors of spacious rooms filled with swarms of busy people, whose perfect workmanship is only excelled by still more perfect implements.

The painters and lacquer-workers were on the third floor—All the main flights of stairs are broad, and so arranged that the banisters may be taken down, and the finished vehicle allowed to slide down in ropes. I especially admired the neat craftsmanship of the harness-workers and upholsterers. We concluded our tour amongst a number of finished coaches, and with an inspection of some fine drawings of all kinds of vehicles.

I was amused to see how the people played into each other's hands, as the saying goes; and that a saddler has a counting house and a paymaster just like a banker.

I should like to have taken the drawing of a coach costing fifteen thousands guineas, made for the Nabob of Arcot, along with me; or that of the Empress of Russia, or Rumbold's, the Governor of the East Indies, —just to have an idea of the size and magnificence of this kind of conveyance.

It was not till three years after the committee's appointment that a book of prices was agreed to. Then it was submitted to consideration by five journeymen, three of them coachmakers and the others harnessmakers and trimmers, who were asked for their observations upon it. To the Company's credit be it said that it brought together employer and employed to settle their differences in a sensible way.

Apart from varying money values it is difficult to give a standard cost for a coach, since different owners required different degrees of elaboration. For example, it is unlikely that the fifth Earl of Bedford would buy the worst, even when he had just succeeded to his property and before he became wealthy. In 1642 we find him* paying Prosser, the coachmaker, £32 10s. 0d. for a new coach and being allowed £5 on his old one. In 1682 £53 10s. 0d. is paid for a new "charet," a lighter vehicle than a coach, but there were serious additions to this: £24 for velvet, £11 for

*Life in a Noble Household, by Miss Scott Thompson, published in 1937.

68

glasses and £14 went to the fringemaker for the "charet and horseclothes." There was a further payment of £30 to Mr. Pink, the painter, whose name, Miss Scott Thompson pleasantly comments, "goes far to justify the invention of the game of 'Happy Families.'"

In 1693 the Earl of Bedford bought another chariot for £43 and this is described as comprising "body, carriage, ironwork, wheels, carving, leather, brass, inside fringe and glasses." Mr. Pink's bill for sumptuous painting of this was £13 15s. 6d.

An interesting description of a coach during the Commonwealth occurs in the "Verney Memoirs."

Sir Ralph was asked by Dr. Denton to obtain a coach for him, and he writes:

PLATE 7
Where several hundred people produced "the loveliest masterpieces of their kind." The premises of John Hatchett (Master, 1785) at 121 Long Acre, London.

> Tell me if you like a coach with one end and a Bed as are used in France, or with 2 ends; ye first is light and holds but 6, the other heavy and holds 8, and soe more apt to breake and kill horses too.

Unfortunately the cost of these vehicles is not disclosed.

We know the price which Mr. Pepys paid for his coach in 1668. After offering £50 he eventually saw the coachmaker "and agreed for £53, and stand to the courtesy of what more I would give him upon the finishing of the coach." The coachmaker's name unluckily is lost, but as he traded in Cow Lane, where so many of the original members of the Company lived, he was certainly one of the body of freemen.

Coming to 1777 it is possible to give a very full invoice for a coach supplied by John Wright and Co. (John Wright was Master of the Company in 1767) to the Rev. John Drake:

1777
Sep. 29. To a new Coach neatly run with raised beads, painted dark green with Arms & Crests, the Leather japan'd and brass beads all round it, lined with fine light colour'd Cloth, trim'd with Velvet Lace the same Colour, the Seat cloth with one row of fringe, plate glasses to slide seperately in front. Plate glasses & Mahogany Shutters in the doors, wainscott Trunks under the Seats, a Carpet to the bottom, hung on a light strong Carriage with iron Axletrees, a new Boot, the Carriage Coach-box to take off the Carriage, & Wheels painted the Colour of the Body 88 0 0

To a Leather Trunk, Iron fastenings, Straps, &c. 3 0 0

To a painted Cloth cover to ditto 12 0

To a Drag chain 10 6

To Dragg staff and Ironwork 6 0

To a new pair of Wheel Harness and Bridles, brass sliders round the Housings, engrav'd brass Crests, screwrings, watering hooks, pollish'd ironwork pipes to the Collars, pollish'd Bitts, Reins' fronts bound and roses		8	0	0
To a best postillion Saddle		1	7	0
To a new leading Rein			2	6
To a new Rein, a yard & half long, with brass buckle to piece out the hand Reins to use with a Phaeton			2	0
To a new pair of Breedoons with double jointed bitts, ye fronts bound			8	6
To a hamper to pack them in			2	6
To packing up the Coachbox with haybands & matting			1	6
To two porters to carry the Coachbox & Harness to ye Inn			2	0
Oct. 6.	To a hammer, pincers, & chizell, 6 lince pins		5	0
Nov. 24.	To a new pair of false Collars	1	4	0

£104 3 6

Recd. Jany. 26, 1778 ye full Contents & all Demands

J^no. WRIGHT.*

In the 18th-century, when no large tools were needed for woodwork, the coachmaker's stock consisted mainly of what is now called work in progress. This is illustrated by the inventories of intestates filed at Guildhall.† One of these relates to the estate of Robert Fawdery, whose name occurs in the Company's Order Books. He died in 1714 and his son Robert was apprenticed to Edmund Harris in February 1716.

The inventory is a lengthy roll of parchment and contains full particulars of the furniture of the house, valued at £61 6s. 6d. "The goods belonging to the trade" deserve to be quoted in full:

*The original of this invoice was presented to the Coachmakers' Company by Captain Tyrwhitt-Drake.

†*Common Serjeant* Book, 6 fo. 7b, in Guildhall Record Office.

In the cellar. A new plain coach body with brass hinges, 2 pair of fore whings, 3 pair of firchells*, 10 extrees†, 6 spring treebars, 1 pair of hind standerds carved, 1 pair of fore and hind standerds uncarved, 12 pieces of elm for foot boards, 18 perches, about 150 foot of wallnutt tree board, 2 transums unfinished & other lumber, and 2 benches to work on

valued at £18–0–2

In the dining room clossetts and cock loftts. 15 door glasses, 5 shorter glasses 5 coach bitts, 4 papers of brass nails, a remnant of green coffoy‡, an old velvett lining, some iron nails, some feathers and feather seals, and some lumber

valued at £18–0–0

In addition to this stock there were three old coaches away from his premises, valued at £29 10s. Then come the entries of the main stock in trade:

In the shop Item. An old carriage and wheels, an old mourning chariott with 4 whole glasses, seats, and box cloath; an old carriage and wheeler; a second hand chariott without lining and glasses, with brass hinges and buckles; a mourning coach, the outside new the inside old, 4 whole glasses, old wheels, iron buckles and hinges; a second hand 2-wheel chase and harness; 21 pair of furchells, 235 extrees, 6 cross barrs, 3 peices of ash 8 foot long, 2 pair of standerds and 1 pair of fore standards and transoms carved, an ashen plank, 72 foot of inch elm, a pair of 2nd hand shaftts, roles and springs, 3 setts & 3 old wheels, 40 pair of firchells, 3 poles made, 60 perches, 7 slit deals, 57 extrees, 49 poles, an old under carriage, 200 of short peices with some standerds, some old iron, wallnuttree board and beech brushes, and hair topings and crops and thongs, and 4 door glasses.

valued at £97–08–00

In the loftt Item. A new plain coach body and 2 new chariott bodys, a chease for a child and odd lumber. In the harness maker's lofft 2 pair of new harness with only brass buckles without headstalls, bitts, lappings, reigns and traces; 48 traces, 10 pair of pole peices, 7 pair of

*Futchell. (*see* footnote in Chapter 6).

†That is, "axle-trees".

‡Possibly the same as "caffa", described by the *Oxford English Dictionary* as a rich, silk, cloth.

collers, 7 pair of hand reigns, 2 pair of coupling reigns, nine bearing reigns, 2 sett of main braces to a length, 4 sett & half cross braces to a length, 20 weather cushions stuffed; 6 very old box clothes and 3 pair of hold hamer clothes, and some very old black and blew cloth, 2 pair of old harness, 30 sawed extrees and some slabbs, 112 course standerds, 44 sawed pillers, 10 transom plates, 36 pole peice buckles, 40 trace rings, 24 coller rings, dees and barrs, 6 dozen of rouel buckles and 12 flank rings, 80 case boxes; an old iron work for a coach body, 6 sides of sadler's leather, one hide of upper leather, 4 hides of Rushia leather, 1 pair of hair toppings; a new cutting board; 2 coach box seats, 4 old leather roofes, 3 hind backs, 6 side windows, 3 pair of cross peices,

PLATE 8
The Lord Mayor of London's magnificent coach was made by Joseph Berry, who was Master of the Coachmakers' Company in 1749.

73

2 pair of brichens [breechings], 8 bassels, 2 housings not
welted, 35 docks and pearch plates, 11 swebar* plates,
1 gross and half of clouts &c.   valued at £72–3–0

There was an unexpired term of 24½ years on the lease of Mr.
Fawdrey's premises in Bishopsgate; he paid £20 per annum rent,
but the real rack rent was estimated at £54 per annum, and the
value in the lease was put at £240:

	£	s.	d.
The total value of all his goods and stock was	586	11	4
and he had in ready money	164	2	6
received from his debtors	385	12	5
	1136	6	3

There were other "debts owing and not received," which
included the somewhat mysterious item "at the warehouse in the
Coachmakers' Society stock . . . . £120," and a group sadly
labelled "esteemed desperate"; these together came to
£613 3s. 10d., and creditors required £607 3s. 1d. After paying
the funeral expenses (£59 5s. 8d.) the estate was therefore a
modest one, and one gathers that coachmaking was not extremely
lucrative in the days of Queen Anne, whom Mr. Fawdery only
just outlived.

*Swebar is for "swivel-bar", to
which the traces of the horses
were attached; the splinter bar
was a later use of a similar
arrangement.

8 The Hall

In 1703, 26 years after the granting of their original Charter, the Coachmakers' Company acquired their own Hall. In the meantime the Court had met in Painter Stainers' Hall by Queenshithe for a time, before moving to the Jewell Chamber at Guildhall and various taverns.

The building which they purchased was in Noble Street and occupied a site that could be traced back to 1400, when Henry IV granted the land, which had been forfeited by Sir Thomas Shelley (a supporter of the Plantagenet Richard II), to one John Dyndon. On this site, in a quiet angle of the City wall, Sir Nicolas Bacon – a Tudor statesman of considerable influence – had built in the 16th-century a house enclosing a small open courtyard in the Tudor style. Bacon House had 20 rooms on the two principal floors, with garrets above. The hall stood on ground to the east; a room nearly as large was at the north and another over the gateway. The long garden had on its south side a covered walk extending the whole length with a gallery above.

In December 1558 Sir Nicolas was appointed Queen Elizabeth's Lord Keeper and left Bacon House to live at Westminster. Two of the later occupants of the house were notable people. William Fleetwood, Recorder of London, lived there from 1574, dating his letters from Bacon House. He was followed by Christopher Barker, the Queen's Printer. Acts of Parliament published by Barker in 1581 and in 1585 bear the words "Imprinted in Bacon House neere Foster Lane". Barker was the first to use Roman typefaces in printing the Bible and he produced 72 editions of the Bible before he died in 1599. Many of these editions were probably printed on the site later occupied by the Coachmakers' Hall.

Bacon House disappeared in the flames of the Great Fire of London in 1666. By that time the house had become Scriveners' Hall. The Scriveners, or Writers, of the Court Letter of the City of London had acquired the property in the troubled reign of King Charles I. Its subsequent destruction was to hit the Scriveners very hard. They rebuilt, with the aid of a mortgage,

75

but being in financial difficulties they were glad, no doubt, to sell the new hall to the Coachmakers Company in May 1703 for the sum of £1,600.

A 51 year lease, at a peppercorn rent, granted the Scriveners the use of the Hall for four days each year for their Court meetings. That was a brotherly courtesy. The transfer of ownership of the Hall was done with due formality. The Coachmakers' Minutes record that . . . .

> . . . . all persons whatsoever being put out of the hall, Mr. Richard Manlove (Master of the Scriveners) re-entered in again and took possession thereof, and then delivered possession thereof to Mr. Jonathan Bentley (Master of the Coachmakers) and Edward Salisbury to ye use of this Company for ever.

Three signatories attested to the transfer. The Court's first order thereafter set up a committee to manage the reconstruction required in the Hall. In the following months a great deal of work was done, the Company paying £120 to Jonathan Maine, the carver; £180 to Daniel Hoskyn, the joiner; and smaller sums to a glazier, plumber, plasterer and smith. Altogether their acquisition, when fitted out to their satisfaction, cost the Company £2,216.

It may be assumed that in 1703 the Coachmakers' Company did not possess an available £1,600 – then a vastly larger sum than the figure represents today. Members loyally built up a fund for the purchase and renovation, contributions coming from 109 of them. As an incentive, the Court passed a resolution to allow all who gave £30 to take and bind an additional apprentice. Certain stock was sold. Still the total was short and the Clerk was instructed to advance the balance of the purchase money, to be repaid to him with interest.

The Coachmakers' Company, at last enjoying a home of their own, held the first Court "at their Hall", as the officers proudly recorded on the 20th May 1703. Perhaps the larger liabilities began to embarrass them, for within three years the Court of Assistants agreed that the Hall might be let to a City Company "but not for a meeting house". The Merchant Taylors made use of the Hall on Lord Mayor's Day. Apart from the actual Hall, kitchen and Beadle's quarters, the premises comprised other rooms, the letting of which brought in revenue . . . .

PLATE 9 (*opposite page*)
The splendid doorway of Coachmakers' Hall in Noble Street, surmounted by the carved and painted coat of arms of the Company.

77

1 Nov. 1728. Mr. Edw. Hopwood, the Company's tennant, applyed for leave for the Gentlemen educated at the Charter house Schoole to have the use of the Co's Hall, kitchen, &c. to dine in on 12 Sept. next . . . . Carried in affirmative, they taking care to have the Hall and other places used by them cleaned and putt in order again.

In the following January, the Poulters' Company offered £15 per annum for the use of the Hall, but this was refused because £20 was the sum demanded by the Coachmakers.

Other tenants appear and disappear. A Mr. King, the Company's tenant in 1731, applied "for leave now and then to dance in the Court Roome at a meeting of private friends, and the Court thought not to grant it".

However, dancing was not to be altogether taboo. Forty odd years later:

8 Jan. 1773. Mr. Richard Hopkins, dancing master, having proposed to take a Lease of the Great Hall and the Rooms over the Beadle's apartments, together with the occasional use of the Great Kitchen for a term of 3 years from Lady Day 1773 at £35 per annum under the Company's usual covenants, the Coy. paying all Taxes and allowing him £2–2–0 towards repairs – Ordered that the Clerk do prepare a Draft of a Lease accordingly.

In 1750 Mr. George Errington offered £50 toward the repairs of the Hall; this was very welcome and, at a later date, the Company signified its gratitude very gracefully:

12 July 1759. George Errington Esq., a member of this Co., and one of the Sherriffes elect, requesting the favour of the use of the Co's Hall on his making his entertainments in his Sherriffalty – and that he also requested a List of the Master & Wardens & their Assistants – it was without debate unanimously order'd that Mr. Errington have the use of the Hall, & a list of the Master, & Wardens, & their Assistants according to his request, and it was further ordered that Mr. Errington have also ye use of ye Co's plate during his Sheriffalty, if he should think proper to use it.

A part of the property, though probably not the Hall, served for a time as an auction room.

Coachmakers' Hall had the invidious distinction of being linked with the Gordon "No Popery" Riots of June, 1780. The prohibition on using the Hall as a meeting place had been withdrawn, no doubt under financial stress. When the Protestant Association was formed to defeat a bill to repeal penalties upon Roman Catholics, it held meetings at Coachmakers' Hall and there the famous resolution of 29th May 1780, which opened the way for rioting, was proposed and carried . . . .

> . . . . that the whole body of the Protestant Association do attend in St. George's Fields, on Friday next at ten o'clock in the morning, to accompany Lord George Gordon to the House of Commons, on the delivery of the Protestant petition.

The fanatical Lord George Gordon was himself present in the Hall. If less than 20,000 of his fellow citizens attended with him the appointed day he would not, he declared, present the petition. Fully 60,000 "true Protestants" answered his call – some would have it there were 100,000, counting the town's riff-raff who had gathered at the opportunity for pillage.

For six days of June 1780, London was given over to mob terror. On the seventh day the riot was put down with loss of life, officially returned as 285 killed and 173 wounded prisoners in the hands of the troops. It is probable, in fact, that the actual casualties exceeded these figures.

In the following year, 1781, a conversation took place:

> *Boswell:* I mentioned a kind of religious Robin Hood Society, which met every Sunday evening at Coachmakers' Hall, for free debate and that the subject for this night was, the text which relates . . . .
> *Johnson* (somewhat warmly): One could not go to such a place to hear it – one would not be seen in such a place – to give countenance to such a meeting . . . .
> *Boswell:* I stole away to the Coachmakers' Hall and heard the difficult text of which we had talked, discussed with great decency and some intelligence by several speakers . . . .

A different use for the Hall was found in the early 19th-century. At its centenary in 1913, the Silver Street Sunday School recalled that 100 years earlier the Coachmakers' Hall had been placed at its disposal, the Hall itself accommodating the boy's school on Sundays. A revival of that honourable use was suggested, but the Court was unable to entertain the application.

In 1842 the Hall was rebuilt and ornamented with decorations from the previous building, but the new Hall evidently did not satisfy the Company for it only stood 28 years.

In 1870 the Hall was pulled down and replaced by a new one with the old panelling refixed and extended where necessary. There were no new features. In order to meet the cost the Company had to raise £3,000 on loan. This charge remained in part until 1935, when a generous gift by Sir Herbert Austin, who had been the Master the year before, cleared off the mortgage and for the first time in more than half a century left the Company free from debt.* The total expenditure on the rebuilding was £3,854.

Within a year of the Court's first assembly in the renovated building, it was threatened with extinction. In 1871 the Mid-London Railway had a bill before Parliament which would have taken not only the Hall, but the whole of the Company's property, which lay adjacent. It was resolved by the Court to petition the House of Lords in opposition should the need arise; but the railway scheme came to nothing.

Associated with the rebuilding of the Hall was a larger scheme which involved the reconstruction of the whole of the Company's property. Until that time, the freehold had been covered by old and dilapidated structures, producing a gross rental of no more than £220 per annum. A firm took the land adjoining the Hall upon lease and thereon erected four warehouses, the result being a welcome accession to the Company's revenue. It was rightly felt that the opportunity for improvement in the Company's own section should not be missed.

Apart from slight damage to the roof (repaired at a cost of £10 15s.) caused by a German bomb falling not far away in a surprise daylight air raid on Saturday morning, 7th July 1917, the Hall remained much the same after the 1870 rebuilding until 1937. Then, the generosity of three past-Masters – Lords Kenilworth (1933), Austin (1934) and Iliffe (1936) – made it

*In the following year, 1936, Sir Herbert was created Lord Austin of Longbridge.

possible to bring the building up to date with a lift, new lighting
and heating and the addition of a dining hall with quarters above
for the Beadle.

The new dining hall permitted the Court to sit down for lunch
after their monthly meetings; up to that time they had sand-
wiches. Court dinners were not introduced until after the Second
World War. The Hall was too small for the annual Livery Dinner,
so this was held in various halls, usually those of the great
companies, and was attended by the Lord Mayor and aldermen.
In 1937 the Livery Dinner was held at the Mansion House, the
Lord Mayor being a guest in his own residence.

An observant passer-by in Noble Street before the Second
World War would have noticed an imposing doorway, with
double doors and the Company's coat of arms above, carved and
painted. That is all he would have seen of the Hall. The Coachmakers' door opened upon a broad passage, apparently tunnelled
through a house belonging to others; actually it was a right of
entry. Old Sir Nicolas Bacon had come that way. At the rear, a
passage branched off at right-angles to stairs and a lift and the
Hall was on the second floor.

It had been brought up from the ground floor on the rebuilding
in 1937 and the new position offered many advantages. Coachmakers' Hall was not so large as others in the City, but it had
height and was cool. A central dome serving as a skylight assured
ample lighting. Arms of 26 of the leading Masters in painted
glass in the windows and the decoration of the dome light with
signs of the Zodiac using designs found at Pompeii – there the
colours were a little strident – reduced the glare and gave the
whole lighting a rosy glow.

The first impression gained was of a pleasant Hall, keeping the
dignity of days long past, yet a little puzzling – till one realised
that the oak screen and panelling, in part, were originals, brought
from the old Hall downstairs. They had been preserved and
replaced in both the later rebuildings of 1842–43 and 1870. The
importance of the screen was attested by the fact that the
Historical Monuments Commission gave it a full page plate in
their survey of monuments in the City*, with this description:

The screen has a middle bay with an elliptical arch
and is flanked by double Corinthian columns supporting

*Inventory of Historical Monu-
ments in London, Volume 4: The
City.

a continuous enriched entablature with a curved and broken pediment; the side bays have Corinthian pilasters.*

The Royal Commission attributed the screen and panelling to *circa* 1703, the year when the Hall was bought from the Scriveners and renovated by the Company. Among the original panelling were noted "four carved panels with pediments and a large panel at the end of the room". Carved achievements of the Royal Stuart arms and those of the Company also figured in the Hall's ornamentation.

The visitor in 1939 would have seen the lists of Masters of the Company and the Clerks, since 1677, painted on the panels in the Hall, while the lists of benefactors were displayed in carved frames bearing the Company's arms in the vestibule as he entered. Since this was dimly lit, the arrangement was not entirely happy.

The Master did not sit in the ancient Master's chair, a venerated relic surrounded and protected by glass. It was made about the year 1670 and was said to have been inherited from the Scriveners' Company. For a long time it was lost. Then, in 1868, Mr. John Winpenny Peters, an Assistant of the Court and past-Master (and a member of the famous coachmaking company) came across it in the possession of a dealer with premises in the George and Catherine Wheel Yard, Bishopsgate Street Without. Peters purchased the chair and presented it to the Company. Artistically, the obvious fault of the chair was over-elaboration, to which was added discomfort. But both for association and craftsmanship it was a valuable period piece.

How the chair came to disappear is not known, but it must have been at a time when furniture and pictures, much regarded and valued today as antiques, were thought of no consequence. For example, the Court of the Coachmakers' Company which met on 2nd August 1838 . . . .

. . . . ordered that the three large pictures and frames in the Hall, be sold for the benefit of the Company.

The three large pictures in question (merit unknown) brought in £4. The same Court placed in the care of the Master the   *See plate 10.*

83

painting entitled *The Picture of Justice*, which was a portrait of George I which Mr. Tovey had presented to the Company in 1727. This painting, also another of the same King and one of Queen Anne, disappeared from the Company's records. The last two pictures had cost the Company £42 in artist's fees. It seems disloyal even to imagine it, but surely these three Royal portraits cannot have been the "three large pictures" which fetched £4 in 1838?

In the ante-room, through which entrance was made to the Hall, there was a tasteful Queen Anne fireplace with moulded and carved surround bearing a festoon of fruit and flowers. The room also contained an oak sideboard with the date 1606 and elaborate carvings and mouldings. It was Flemish work, presented by an unknown donor. But the gem of the Company's smaller possessions, apart from the plate, was undoubtedly the Poor Box of 1680.

The Poor Box was shown at the City Companies Exhibition, staged in 1927 at the Victoria and Albert Museum, where it attracted attention and was illustrated in the official catalogue. Isaac Nicks was the carver and donor. He does not appear to have been a freeman of the Company. Small enough to handle and pass round, the Poor Box has carved figures of the Four Evangelists standing at the corners – a delightfully conceived and executed piece of craftsmanship.

The ante-room also contained the Company's little library. In 1868 a committee of the Court prepared a list of books as suitable to form the nucleus of a collection for reference. First gifts were made by George N. Hooper and William Hooper – names honoured in the trade – with the hope of encouraging others. Among their gifts was an album of carriage drawings by Samuel Hobson, who, with his brother Henry, was probably the most influential coachmaker of the 19th-century in matters of design and construction. All members had access to the library. Drawings and prints of coaches, horses and harness, many of great rarity, old coaching waybills and photographs of past-Masters overflowed on to the staircase.

In 1932 the Company accepted a gift of old pictures and catalogues from Peters and Sons, the famous coachmakers who had made many vehicles for the Royal Family. A few months later it was decided to clean up the library and make it usable for committee meetings. A list of "unwanted" books (including Thrupp's two volume *History of Coaches*), engravings and photographs was prepared and they were then offered to any members who cared to collect them. This would seem to have been a lamentable dispersal of valuable coachmaking records, except that it at least saved them – unwittingly – from the certain destruction that would have befallen them eight years later if they had stayed in the Company's possession.

When war was declared on 3rd September 1939, the City of London braced itself for immediate attack by German bomber aircraft, but a year was to pass before any serious damage occurred. In the meantime, the Company decided to close the Hall (to avoid paying rates), store the furniture and dispense with the services of the Beadle. While inquiries were still being made about storage accommodation, Fate overtook the Company.

On Saturday, 7th September 1940, frustrated in his endeavour to sweep the Royal Air Force from the skies before invading Britain, Hitler switched his bomber force to sustained night raids on London. What became known as the Blitz went on for 75 consecutive nights, causing immense destruction by high explosive and fire. The Court met for the last time in the Company's Hall in October. The Beadle was summoned before the Court and was reprimanded; some of the dust caused by the bombing of the previous weeks had not been completely swept from the tables in the Court Room.* Soon there were to be no tables to dust.

The air raids became intermittent, but no less intense, reaching a climax on the night of Sunday, 29th December 1940. In Winston Churchill's words:

> It was an incendiary classic. The weight of the attack was concentrated upon the City of London itself. It was timed to meet the dead low-water hour. The water mains were broken at the outset by very heavy high-explosive parachute mines. Nearly 1,500 fires had to be fought . . . . Eight Wren churches were destroyed or damaged. The Guildhall was smitten by fire and blast and St. Paul's Cathedral was only saved by heroic exertions. A void of ruins at the very centre of the British world gapes upon us to this day.†

*It is perhaps worth mentioning that only the Master and three Assistants were present; there were 23 absentees.

†Churchill was writing in 1950: *The Second World War*, Volume 2: *Their Finest Hour*.

That void was caused by the greatest conflagration of the six major fires that – as well as 16 others – have come to be known as The Great City Fire.

Coachmakers' Hall was engulfed by it. So, too, were the Company's adjacent premises. All were gutted, as the immediate past-Master, Vincent Alford and the Clerk, James Smith, found when they were able to see what was left of the Hall on Tuesday 31st December. The only way to reach it was on foot. The approach roads and pavements were strewn with abandoned fire-hoses and debris. Noble Street itself was two feet deep in rubble and the buildings were still smouldering. From the ruins of the Hall they rescued a kitten, singed but still alive.

The Company's plate, together with the model of the Royal State Coach, had previously been moved from the Hall, but the greater part of the Company's possessions including the Master's chair, the library of books, prints and photographs and some early Minute Books were destroyed in the fire. Alford and Smith were able to recover the Company's Charter, but the document containing the Orders, Rules and Ordinances of the Company was missing. It had evidently been removed by some unauthorised person because some years after the war, in 1955, it was offered to the Company by a bookseller, Rothschild Davidson of Monmouth Street. He had acquired it together with a number of second-hand books from a garage in Camden Town, which had been used by the Auxiliary Fire Service during the war.

The office seals of the Lord High Chancellor, the Lord Treasurer and the Lord Chief Justice of the Court of Common Pleas, which had originally been appended beneath their respective signatures, were missing when the document was recovered. These seals had been enclosed in skippets, or capsules, of ivory held by silken cords which had evidently been cut. The margins of the six sheets of sheepskin comprising the document had been eaten in places by rats, but otherwise it was in good order. After a preliminary examination by the Clerk, past-Master Vincent Alford took Dr. Albert Hollander, the archivist of Guildhall, to inspect the document. Dr. Hollander pronounced its authenticity "beyond all doubt". One reason was that the document was in its original receptacle, one of three rectangular tin boxes made and inscribed uniformly at the beginning of the 19th-century to hold the Charter, an emblazoned exemplification of the grant of arms,

PLATE 11 (*opposite page*)
All that remained of the Hall after the incendiary bombs had done their work in 1940.

86

and the ordinances. Dr. Hollander added that the document was of first importance from the archivist's point of view. The Company were extremely fortunate in being able to acquire it for £20. All these documents are now in the safe-keeping of the Archives Room at Guildhall.

In the same year, 1955, the Society of Genealogists informed the Company that they had in their possession a book containing a record of all apprentices of the Company, from 1677 to 1800. The Company had no record of apprentices for the years 1677 to 1727, so a typewritten copy was obtained from the Society.

The Hall was no more, but the business of the Company had to go on. This was the signal for a spontaneous display of the fellowship that binds the Livery Companies together. The first to offer sympathy and help were the Leathersellers, and they were quickly followed by the Vintners, the Tallow Chandlers, the Plumbers, the Haberdashers, the Wax Chandlers, the Saddlers and the Dyers. In the end, the offer of the Vintners to provide a room for meetings of the Court at their hall in Upper Thames Street was accepted with gratitude. Later on the Court met at Tallow Chandlers' Hall in Dowgate Street.

Immediately after the war there was a move to build a Common Hall on the site of the Salters' Hall, to be shared by the Salters with the other Companies that had lost their halls in the war – the Coachmakers, the Carmen, the Cordwainers, the Wheelwrights, the Farriers, the Loriners, the Paviours and the Shipwrights. But some of the Companies already had plans of their own and nothing came of it.

In 1950 the Company decided in principle to rebuild Coachmakers' Hall on the Noble Street site, subject to agreement being reached with the Scriveners about a small piece of land. The scheme did not look so attractive however, when the estimated cost was found to be £170,000. Therefore, when the Company were told by the Corporation of London in 1954 that their site was scheduled for compulsory purchase, they decided not to object but to accept the offer of £17,500 in compensation. They had already received £3,000 (less the value of goods at the bank and the solicitors) for the goods and chattels from the War Damage Commission.

Shelley House now occupies the approximate site of the Hall in Noble Street; and on part of the site of the warehouses owned by the Company in Oat Lane stands the rebuilt Pewterers' Hall.

9 Carriages in the 19th-century

WITH the improvement in roads and the springing of vehicles at the end of the 18th-century, coachmakers were able to produce lighter carriages in much greater variety.

The first of these appeared in 1788 and was called the Phaeton – why, nobody seems to know. There were two types of Phaeton to begin with, the High Perch and the Crane Neck, both being described generally as High-flyers on account of their tall wheels and high bodies, which made them at once dangerous and attractive for the young men, led by the Prince of Wales (later King George IV) who suddenly discovered the pleasure of driving. For the details of these vehicles, and those that follow, the Company is indebted to Mrs. Marylian Watney, whose delightful and authoritative book, *The Elegant Carriage*, is a comprehensive and concise survey of many types of horse-drawn vehicles.

The first practical light carriage was the Italian-designed Curricle, which also received the patronage of the Prince of Wales and came on the scene at the turn of the century. It had the distinction of being the only two-wheeled vehicle drawn by a pair. Famous owners of Curricles included the Duke of Wellington and Charles Dickens. It was largely superseded by the single horse-power French Cabriolet, which differed from the Curricle in having only a small platform behind for the groom instead of the Phaeton's seat. The groom was called a "tiger" because of his striped waistcoat, and it was fashionable for him to be as diminutive as possible.

The early, excessively high Phaetons were replaced in the 19th-century by much lower vehicles which were produced in great variety, from the Pony Phaeton made for George IV to the great Mail Phaeton of 1828. There were also Park Phaetons, Spider and Ladies' Phaetons – indeed all four-wheeled carriages were called Phaetons, type names being added when they were made to special order, such as Albert, Beatrice, Beaufort, Emperor, Empress, Eugene, Siamese, Vienna, Victoria and Scarborough.

The term Victoria seems to have been applied to two vehicles. In 1828 a Pony Phaeton drawn by four ponies ridden postillion was made for the Princess Victoria, and in 1851 as Queen she had a smaller copy made by Andrews of Southampton which became known as the Victoria. The second type of Victoria appeared 18 years later. On a visit to Paris in 1869 the Prince of Wales was so taken by a hackney vehicle called the Milord, which had been imported from England, that he brought one back with him. After receiving the Royal approval it was thereafter called the Victoria. With its low-hung body and ease of entry (there were no doors) it became a fashionable vehicle, especially in the summer.

The most unusual Phaeton was called the "Equirotal" and was described by notable past-Master of the Coachmakers' Company, George Thrupp, in his *History of Coaches* published in 1877. It comprised in effect two vehicles, a Gig in front being attached by pivots to a Curricle or Cabriolet at the rear. The driver's seat thus

PLATE 12
*"The Turn Out of the Season".
Count d'Orsay driving his curricle
past the statue of Achilles in Hyde
Park.*

turned with the front wheels, and this kept him squarely behind the horse at all times.

Then there was the Gig, which started life as a plebeian vehicle often hired out by coachbuilders to avoid the tax on new carriages. Later it moved up in the world and was used by the rich as well, as exemplified by the Stanhope Gig (1815) made by Tilbury. Other popular Gigs were the Liverpool and the Lawton, made by a coachmaker who at the end of the century produced a hooded Gig called the Buggy – a name adopted by the Americans for light vehicles of various types. And there were Cars and Carts of all kinds, the best known being the Dog Cart of *circa* 1800 (the Governess Cart did not appear until 100 years later). There were many variations of the Dog Cart – the Eridge, Oxford, Windsor, Reading, Newport Pagnell, Bedford, Leicester, Craven, etc., etc.

At the other end of the scale was the Private Drag, in reality a private coach on the lines of a Mail Coach which was used by gentlemen for four-in-hand driving and was particularly useful at race meetings, when it also served as a private grand stand.

The development of light carriages was given a great impetus in 1805 by Obadiah Elliott's patent for elliptic springs, which enabled the heavy wooden or iron perch and cross-beds to be dispensed with and at the same time gave the occupants a smoother ride. For this invention Elliott was awarded the gold medal of the Society of Arts in 1820 after a committee of 37 of its members had visited his works in Westminster Bridge Road and had carefully and thoroughly tested a carriage fitted with his springs. Nevertheless many carriages continued to be suspended on an iron perch with under- and C-springs and leather braces which gave an even softer ride.

The design of coachmen-driven carriages also changed a great deal in the early part of the 19th-century. The first big advance was the Landau, which originated in Germany and was introduced in England by a coachbuilder named Luke Hopkinson, who was Master of the Coachmakers in 1822. The Landau was a convertible, and in Hopkinson's Briska-Landau the two hoods could be folded flat while at the same time the seats rose six inches to give the occupants a better view. The Barouche, another German design, started as a heavy, low-slung vehicle that in due course became a smart equipage which was in as much demand as a sporting vehicle (when it was owner-driven) as it was as a

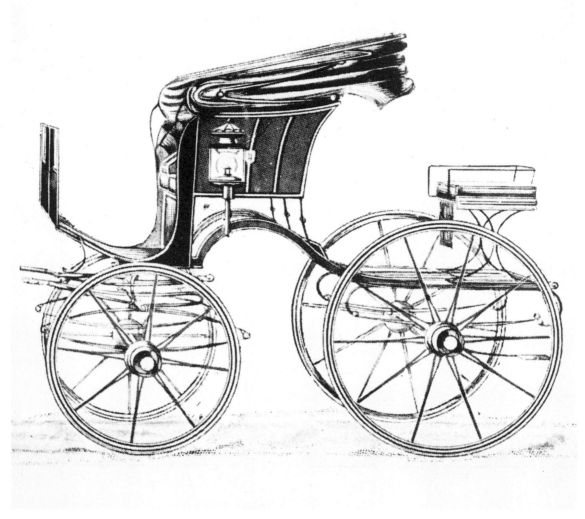

town carriage with a pair, four or even six horses. In 1835 another popular town carriage, the Milord (the forerunner of the Victoria) was introduced by David Davies of Albany Street, the man who was responsible for the first Hackney Cabriolet (the origin of the "cab") that appeared in London in 1823.

Two years after the Milord appeared on the streets, Queen Victoria ascended to the throne as a young princess. The Coachmakers' Company was caught up in the hopeful enthusiasm of the times. In order to create the least possible disturbance of

PLATE 13
A Spider Phaeton built by Hooper in the early part of the 19th-century.

the City's activities Her Majesty decided that Lord Mayor's Day should also be the occasion of her own State visit to Guildhall. Letters came from the Town Clerk, and the Coachmakers were quick with their loyal response. "Standing" – the old civic term, actually seating – for 50 of the officers and Livery of the Company was obtained from the Dean and Chapter of St. Paul's within the churchyard rails on the south side. On this auspicious 9th of November 1837 as the young Queen passed, they can be pictured there, marshalled according to seniority. The Coachmakers' stand, roofed with red and blue drapery (not blue and yellow, as might have been expected), bore on its front the carved arms of the Company, regilt for the occasion, and from various points flags and banners floated. As darkness fell in early evening, lamps were lighted to form a crown at the summit of the stand. There were also stars, and the letters V and R. At the banquet given in Guildhall the Company's plate appeared on the sideboard.

It is worth lingering over this honourable observance, for it was to be the last. When Queen Victoria visited the City with Prince Albert on 28 October 1844 to open the rebuilt Royal Exchange, the Coachmakers' Company did not ask for a standing. On the arrival of Princess Alexandra of Denmark to marry the Prince of Wales in 1863 the Master and Wardens rode in the procession through the City in a carriage drawn by four horses with postillions, and attended by banner men – indeed the Coach-makers fittingly headed the Mayoral *cortège* as it left Guildhall to meet the Royal bride across London Bridge. But by the time the long reign ended in 1901 the City Companies had lost the practice of being represented *en masse* on important civic occasions. It seems a pity that some of these public appearances are not revived. The Lord Mayor's Show each year gives the only opportunity for the sight-seeing public to be made aware of the City Companies' useful existence.

The best known and most widely used of all Victorian carriages, the Brougham, came into being in 1838. The Company is fortunate in having the original vehicle in its possession (it is in store at the Science Museum, South Kensington). How this happened, and the history of the vehicle, are worth recording in some detail.

In 1894 Earl Bathurst wrote to the Company from Cirencester House, Gloucestershire, saying that he believed he had the famous vehicle in his coach house and offering it to the Company

PLATE 14

The Victoria, a fashionable town carriage based on the earlier Milord designed by David Davies of Albany Street.

as a gift. George N. Hooper, a coachmaker of distinction and a past-Master of the Company, went down and cast an expert eye over the vehicle. He confirmed its authenticity. It was indeed the identical carriage in which not only Lord Chancellor Brougham but Gladstone and Disraeli had also ridden.★

The announcement of the Company's acquisition led to some discussion about the vehicle, from which it emerged that in 1838 Lord Brougham had instructed his coachmakers, the firm of Sharp & Bland of South Audley Street, to make him a private version of the four-wheel cab carrying two passengers inside and one on the box seat which had recently been introduced on the London streets. But such a vehicle was outside the run of carriages made by Sharp & Bland, who specialised in larger vehicles like Barouches and Landaus, so the Lord Chancellor turned to another firm in Mayfair, Robinson & Cook of Mount Street, Grosvenor Square, to carry out his wishes. The Brougham

★*See plate 17.*

94

made by Robinson & Cook had no steps to the body and had a sword case behind, as was usual with all carriages built at that time when highwaymen were still one of the perils of travelling. It also had a large and strong guard (or "opera") board behind to protect the occupants from injury from the thrust of the pole of any following vehicle that was being recklessly driven. The carriage was painted light olive green, a fashionable colour at the time.

The original Brougham was the result of collaboration between Lord Brougham and Robinson & Cook, but he did not buy it and the firm jobbed it to him for two years. In 1840 a second vehicle with various improvements was made and became the property of Lord Brougham. The original Brougham was sold to Sir William Foulis of Inglesby Manor, Stokesley, Yorkshire, and it afterwards passed into the hands of Lord Henry Bentinck and Lord Bathurst as owners in turn.

Lord Brougham's carriage was so much admired that it was immediately copied by many other coachmakers, among the first to do so being George Thrupp, grandson of Joseph Thrupp, who had started the business in 1760. The Brougham was made

PLATE 15
The Mail Coach, with changes of horses every ten miles, provided fast travel with the utmost regularity – people set their clocks by its passage.

in thousands and was popular throughout the reign of Queen
Victoria.

Whereas the Brougham was essentially a sober and dignified
conveyance, the Hansom Cab always had a rather romantic air
about it (Disraeli called it the Gondola of London). Actually the
vehicle invented by Mr. Hansom in 1834 was quite different from
the Hansom Cab that afterwards became a part of the London
scene. It never went into service and the Hansom Cab as we think
of it today was the result of John Chapman completely redesign-
ing Hansom's prototype. The Hansom was of course a two-
wheeler, but a four-wheel cab for two passengers inside and one
one the box seat beside the driver quickly followed. This was the
inspiration of Lord Brougham's idea for a small private carriage.
A four-wheel closed carriage to seat four, bigger than the
Brougham but smaller than the Town Coach, was introduced in
1842 by Laurie & Marner of Oxford Street. This was the Clarence

(sometimes called the Sovereign or Carriole), which was of such a useful size that it was also made as a four-wheel cab, in which form it earned the nick-name "Growler" on account of its noise.

Another vehicle that became part of the English language was the Wagonette, which was first made in England in 1842 by Lovell, a coachmaker at Amersham in Buckinghamshire, to the order of Lord Curzon, who lived nearby at Penn. The Wagonette

PLATE 17
An historic vehicle – the first Brougham, made by Robinson and Cook for the Lord Chancellor. It was presented to the Company in 1894 by Earl Bathurst and is kept at the Science Museum, London.

was the ideal vehicle for family excursions in the countryside. It was soon being turned out by other coachmakers, Holmes of Derby making one for the Earl of Chesterfield and Hoopers of London building one for Queen Victoria in 1845 under the personal supervision of Prince Albert. The Wagonette was essentially an aristocratic vehicle, later versions being called Portland and Lonsdale after their noble owners. A larger vehicle on the same lines called the Char-à-Banc was presented to Queen Victoria by King Louis-Philippe in 1844. Its rows of seats, all facing forward, made it just as useful as a sight-seeing vehicle as it was for carrying shooting parties, and it was in this form that it survived as an open motor vehicle into the 1920s. Another French vehicle, the Fourgon (luggage van) was used to carry servants and their master's baggage. A variation of the Wagonette was the Brake (or Break, as it was sometimes spelt) used for carrying staff and equipment, especially on sporting occasions.

For longer journeys by the well-to-do a variety of carriages was produced in the early 19th-century, beginning with the Travelling Chariot made by T. G. Adams in 1815. This was virtually a Post-Chaise and was hired with post-boys to ride the

PLATE 18
The Brougham was copied by many coachbuilders. This is Hooper's "improved" version, drawn by J. Gilfoy.

horses, which were usually supplied by the hirer for the initial stages. The Britchka, an Austrian vehicle which appeared three years later, was a private travelling carriage which could be converted to a full-length bed at night and was consequently popular with King's Messengers on their journeys carrying diplomatic bags. A somewhat similar vehicle was the Dormeuse made by Adams & Hooper, who supplied one to the Duke of Beaufort.

An original carriage which appeared in 1851, the year of the Great Exhibition, was the Dioropha, made by Rock & Hawkins of Hastings (Rock was a liveryman). It was a dual purpose vehicle with interchangeable heads, open or closed, rather like the hardtop arrangement of the sports car of a century later. The head was hoisted up by means of a pulley on the coach-house ceiling.

Meanwhile improvements in the design of carriages and coaches had not stopped with Obadiah Elliott. In 1820 Samuel

PLATE 19
The Balmoral Sociable, in which Queen Victoria drove over the St. Gotthard and Furka passes in Switzerland in 1868. It was built by Cook and Holdaway, successors to Robinson and Cook, who made the original Brougham, and is now at the Royal Mews, Buckingham Palace. Both Robinson and Cook became Masters of the Coach-makers' Company.

PLATE 20

Part of the collection of armorial bearings presented to the Company in 1950 by the widow of Horace Nutt, head of the famous coach-making firm, Barkers. Geoffrey Smith enabled the Company to have them suitably preserved.

Hobson, who had been trained by the famous firm of Barker, showed how smaller wheels (3ft. 3in. in front and 4ft. 5in. behind) could improve the shape of a vehicle, while in 1851 Hoopers came out with a new method of suspension by means of a single wrought-iron perch and horizontal springs which enabled the wheels and axles to be made lighter.

Although they were used mostly for short journeys in town and country, private carriages of the 19th-century often travelled long distances. An account of such a journey – from London to Taunton – is to be found in *Annals of the Road*, produced by Capt. Malet, XIIIth Hussars, in 1876. In an extract, entitled *A Drive on the Great Western Road*, reprinted below, Malet praises the inns and the service they provide, and goes on to describe his vehicle and horses. Except in towns and villages he would have met few other vehicles, and he could proceed at his own pace without danger or harassment. Although the road and the traffic have changed completely since then, the inns survive a century later – all bar one of those mentioned in this extract are recommended by the RAC and the AA in their 1976 Guides.

A DRIVE ON THE GREAT WESTERN ROAD

My experience of the Great Western Road, from driving down to Taunton two or three years ago, enables me to speak highly in its favour. The road is kept in excellent order throughout, and the inns are well kept and most comfortable. In all the inns I put up at, post-horses are kept. I give them as I found them.

The 'Virginia Water' inn, excellent accommodation for man; but as I only changed horses here, cannot say what accommodation they may have for horses. The Hartford Bridge inn we found shut up. At Basingstoke, the 'Red Lion', capital stables and good in every way. Andover, the 'Star and Garter' inn, all very good indeed; the tits (contemporary term for horses) in the stable well looked after. Park House inn, only baited (gave food to horses) here. Salisbury, the 'White Hart', excellent. Blandford, the 'Crown', very good. Woodgate's inn shut up, Mr. Day having taken the inn as part of his extensive stables; though if a feed of oats is all you require, I feel sure it would not be denied you. I remember being shown in this inn, some years ago, a three-legged table in a parlour, each leg of which stood in a different county! Mr. Day's racing-stables are in themselves worth going all this way to view. At Sherborne, the 'Digby'. This inn has taken the place of the 'King's Arms', and no words of mine can sufficiently praise this establishment, for in truth stables and house are in themselves a model of perfection. The 'Antelope' too is an excellent inn here with good stables. As on my return journey I stayed at Sherborne to hunt, I can speak with some knowledge of the inns. I should like to speak of the 'Leicestershire of the South' as a hunting country, but I must get on the road again and merely say *en passant*, 'try it'. At Ilminster, the 'George', everything very good; Taunton, the 'Castle', excellent.

For the benefit of those who may wish to travel as we

did, I may state how we went. Horses, a pair of brown geldings 15'2, short in leg, light in mouth with plenty of bone and barrel; they could do their mile in four minutes easy. The carriage (a Stanhope Phaeton with a hood) was hung on telegraph springs, an imperial (luggage trunk) fitted under the fall of the hood behind, and overhanging the body to the breadth of the front seat, strapped to a dee on either side under the body, another narrow imperial strapped on to the front dash, and the groom's box fitted under the hind seat. The 'three feet of tin' (horn), a necessity on long journeys, hung at my whip hand in its basket. I never enjoyed anything more than this and other similar travels in my life.

In 1870 the 30-year-old Rev. Francis Kilvert was appointed curate at Clyro in Radnorshire, where he stayed for seven years. Throughout these years he kept a diary vividly recording life in the Victorian countryside, in which carriages of various kinds played an important part.

These extracts are reproduced from *Kilvert's Diary, 1870–1879*, edited by F. R. Fletcher and published for the first time in the years 1938 to 1940 by Jonathan Cape Limited.

Wednesday, 9 February 1870

A very cold night and a slight shower of snow fell early this morning. Then it froze all day. The mountains all white . . . . Went with the Venables to dine at Whitney Court, driving in the mail phaeton and sitting behind with Charlie. Bitterly cold with a keen E. wind but we were well wrapped up and the hood kept the wind off us . . . . A grand night with stars glittering frosty keen and we came home at a rattling pace.

Friday 11 February 1870

Baskerville in his brougham with the old bay cob came to the door at 6.3. Very cold drive. Mrs. Bevan, Mary, and the Crichtons arrived before us all in Mrs. Allen's yellow chariot . . . . It was a very happy evening.

Tuesday 22 February 1870

Mrs. V. went out for a drive, on the Rhayader road, the carriage and cushions thoroughly aired and warmed with hot water bottles and a warming pan.

Thursday 24 February 1870

Writing a sermon for Ash Wednesday. Dined with Mrs. V., who drove down with Brewer from Llysdinam in the yellow Perthcart with the grey mare this afternoon. A lovely evening and the Black Mountain lighted up grandly, all the furrows and water courses clear and brilliant . . . . A market woman's chestnut horse restive in the road and market folk on foot winding their way home through the fields by Wyeside.

Tuesday 29 March 1870

Home at 6, dressed for dinner. At 6.30 Charles with the mail phaeton and the two mares, grey and bay, dashed up to the door in grand style. I was ready and away we went to the Vicarage to pick up the Vicar, who took the reins. At Peter's Pool we overtook and passed at a dashing pace the Clyro Court brougham with one horse wherein were the Squire and Mr. Frank Guise, the recorder of Hereford, bound like ourselves for dinner at Oakfield. It was refreshing to see the Vicar's stylish equipage driven by himself with two servants behind, dashing past the small humble turn-out of the Squire, rather reversing the usual order of things.

Thursday, 7 July 1871

It was a very pleasant dinner . . . . good champagne and the first salmon I have tasted this year . . . . Clifford Priory is certainly one of the nicest and most comfortable houses in this part of the country. The evening was exquisite and the party wandered out into the garden promiscuously after dinner under the bright moon, which shone alone in the unclouded sky. When the party re-assembled in the drawing room there was music . . . . Mr. Allen brought me as far as Hay in the rumble of his most antiquated, most comfortable old yellow chariot on C springs, very large, broad and heavy and able to carry 7 people. We had 6 on board, Mrs. Allen, Thomas and Pope inside – I preferred the night air and the tramping of the fast mare. Going up the hills we had before us the antiquated figure of the old coachman against the sky and amongst the stars. So we steadily rumbled into Hay and there was a great light in the North shewing where the sun was travelling along below the horizon, and only just below.

THE first half of the 19th-century saw the Company slowly decline in influence. It was forced to recognise that the old order had changed, that some of the powers it formerly exercised had dropped away, and others could no longer be enforced. For example, the power of search, by which control of the trade had largely been exercised, lapsed before the 18th-century was out, owing to the constant friction it occasioned and the unpopularity of a duty which set members of the Company and of the trade to spy upon one another. In addition, there was every-increasing difficulty in obtaining the warrant for search by the Lord Chief Justice, which the Charter required.

By the Charter, no one could lawfully carry on the trade of a coachmaker or coach harness maker within London and Westminster and 20 miles around without being a member of the Company. In early times the Company sought to enforce this right with the result that the men attacked generally came into its fold and authority. But ultimately any attempt made to compel enrolment met with resistance; there were no corporate funds with which to contest a legal issue, and the claim was allowed to lapse by disuse. The limitation of apprentices had kept down the number of workmen and made the trade a closed one. This was abrogated by a new by-law passed in 1804, which left unrestricted the numbers that any master coach-builder or coach harness maker might take.

The plain fact was that the Company could legislate for the trade no longer. A standing committee was appointed by the Company to watch all matters connected with the taxation of carriages and matters prejudicial to the interests of the trade. The setting up of a board of arbitration in the coachmaking industry was considered and was rejected, mainly because of the wide diversities of price, style and quality of the article produced, and the varying condition of purchase and hire.

From the administrative point of view the Company apparently fell into a scandalous state of inefficiency. According to George

Hooper, who joined in 1867, it was a "worn out and effete Guild which had drifted into a wretched chaos of mismanagement." With three other coachmakers, James Robinson, John Woodall and Henry Mountford Holmes, he set about putting things straight. "Its register of members and quarterage book had been so neglected," he wrote later, "that it showed quarterage payments 10, 20, 30, 40 and in one case 80 years in arrears. Most of these arrears were against members who had long been dead, but whose names had never been removed from the register." George Hooper and his henchmen became Assistants of the Court within four years of joining and Hooper was elected Master three years later, by which time the internal management of the Company had been restored to a reputable state.

Hooper's strictures did not apply to the external work of the Company. With the power of trade unions and employers' organisations steadily usurping its traditional functions, and lacking the large endowments of some of the older Livery Companies for charitable work, the Company believed there was a task to be done in improving the design and workmanship of carriages. A start was made in 1865 when the free use of the Hall was given to the Operative Coachmakers' Industrial Exhibition, which was opened by the Marquis of Landsdowne and for which the Company presented medals. The Master himself, Thomas How, gave a prize of five guineas for the best design of an open and closed carriage. One of the Company's medals was awarded for "an odometer, or carriage distance indicator", and another was for "a model wagonette with Morgan's patent machinery to open and close by a screw worked by the driver whilst in the coach-box."

From then on the awarding of medals, certificates of honour and money prizes became a regular part of the Company's activities and covered the whole trade of coachmaking – body makers, carvers, joiners, spring makers, smiths, vicemen, painters, herald painters, wheelers, trimmers, harness makers, lace makers, lamp makers, platers, chasers, sawyers – in all cases the description being preceded by the word Coach.

The Coachmakers were the first of the City Guilds to promote modern technical education. This escaped the notice of a luckless Lord Mayor (Alderman Dakin) who stated in a speech delivered in 1871 that the Turners' Company had taken the initiative in technical education and presenting medals, and expressed his wish to see other Companies following so good a lead. The Master of the Coachmakers reminded the Lord Mayor that this Company had annually since 1865 offered money prizes in connection with the examination of the Government Department of Science and Art, had awarded medals, and that year was giving medals and money prizes for drawings of carriages or parts of carriages to scale, by freemen and journeymen and apprentice coachmakers. For once the traditional Mansion House courtesy failed; the letter drew no acknowledgement.

(The breach lasted for some years, but it was healed by time. In 1879 the drawings and models in the annual competition were shown for some days at the Mansion House, where the Lord Mayor distributed the prizes given by the Coachmakers' Company in public competition as well as to students of the coach-making classes it supported. Later the Baker Street Carriage Bazaar was a favourite place for exhibition.)

The competitions were mainly for drawings or models of specific vehicles – for example, a sporting Phaeton or a four-wheeled Dog Cart; a double-seated Victoria with or without doors; a square Landau with high boot, hung on elliptic springs; a four-in-hand Coach; or a Skeleton double cab-shaped Sociable with driving seat supported on elegant open iron-work. In 1884 drawings were required for "a ladies driving Phaeton, ascent between the wheels, any shape (except Stanhope or Mail) eligible, the hood to be shown down." Three years later the awards were for (1) a single Brougham on perch carriage, (2) an undersprung Victoria Phaeton, (3) an elliptic spring Landau, canoe-shaped. Apart from these awards for complete vehicle designs, special prizes were offered for the best essay or treatise on the making of carriage bodies (20 guineas in this case), on axles, springs and iron-work, the best height of wheels, and on carriage painting, varnishing and trimming.

In 1871 the Company had the bright idea of sending a team of previous medal winners to the Paris Exhibition to report on various aspects of the coachwork exhibits – coach body making, coach wheels and undercarriages, coach smithing and spring making, trimming work, coach painting, exterior iron-work, interior fittings, coach lamps, coach and harness plating, and coach chasing.

This initiative was repeated for the 1878 Paris Exhibition. The Company paid each person selected the sum of five pounds in advance to cover his expenses to and from Paris and a further five pounds after the receipt of his written report in London. The personal arrangements were made in conjunction with the Society of Arts and included suitable lodgings for 16 shillings a week in advance. Good dinners, "served as in England", could be obtained at 1s. 3d., or three meals a day for three shillings at the Workman's Hall near the Exhibition.

A special arrangement was made with the South East and London, Chatham and Dover Railway for a return ticket to Paris at the price of 20 shillings in exchange for a certificate from the Society of Arts. Each artisan was furnished with a route card "by means of which he will be recognised at the railway stations and this will entitle him to attention from guards and other officials." In Paris the party had the help of a British interpreter.

The French were naturally the largest exhibitors with 180 carriages standing in four rows (they had applied for 800 spaces). The British were next with a fine display of Drags, Landaus, Barouches, Broughams, Victorias, Stanhope and Park Phaetons, Dog Carts (the most numerous) and Gigs. William Heywood of Huntingdon, one of the visiting team, reported:

> The finest exhibit of small, light, strong carriages is by Windover. The lines are striking, well proportioned and well finished. The finest specimens of work in large carriages are by Cockshoot, Peters, McNaught & Smith, Henderson, Adelbert, Holmes, and Mulliner .... The perch of Cockshoot and the under carriages of McNaught & Smith are fine specimens of forging, and the fittings are not surpassed by any in the English Department.

The distinction of Chevalier of the Legion of Honour was conferred upon John Winpenny Peters, of the firm of Peters & Sons of London, who had been Master of the Company in 1858. Cockshoots were awarded a gold medal, Henderson, Holland & Holland, H. & A. Holmes, McNaught & Smith, F. Mulliner, Peters, Thorn and Wyburn all won silver medals, while H. Mulliner, Rock & Hawkins and Windover were awarded bronze medals.

London, of course, had its International Exhibitions too and in 1873 the Duke of Edinburgh (Queen Victoria's son, later the reigning Duke of Saxe-Coburg-Gotha) was chairman of the exhibition. He wrote saying that "he appreciated the importance of obtaining the cordial assistance of the great City Companies. With satisfaction he had learnt that the Coachmakers' Company would co-operate in securing a good representation of the carriage-building trades." The Company did more; it contributed £50.

Learning that the Duke of Edinburgh would favourably receive a nomination for membership, the Company at a special Court held on the 7th February 1873 passed a resolution that the freedom and livery be presented, and that his Royal Highness be elected to the Court of Assistants. Room was made for him by the voluntary resignation of Frederic Chancellor from the Court. (He was re-elected at the next vacancy, without fees.) The Duke of Edinburgh, who came to Coachmakers' Hall with his equerries, was thereupon introduced to the Court, on which he was to remain till his death. He passed to his seat after taking the customary oaths. *Déjeuner* followed in the Hall, attended by the Lord Mayor (Sir Sidney Waterlow) and no fewer than 23 past-Masters. After the Master proposed the toast of the Duke (saluted by the band of the West London Rifles playing "Rule Britannia" in recognition of the Duke being a naval officer), the Duke proposed the toast of the Master (at which the band burst into "The Fine old English Gentleman"). The Master that year was Henry Mountford Holmes, of the old-established firm of carriage builders, H. and A. Holmes of London, Derby and Lichfield. Every officer present on the occasion was a master coachmaker.

In his speech the Master informed the Royal Duke that though attendance at the Court of Assistants was prescribed, it was only to such extent as would not interfere with other primary engagements. Nevertheless the proper form was observed and in the minutes of succeeding meetings the Duke of Edinburgh figured among "absentees this day."

The year of the enrolment of the Duke of Edinburgh in the Court of Assistants was made additionally notable by the accession to the Company of a famous Prime Minister. Benjamin Disraeli, when approached, expressed his willingness to accept the freedom and the livery of the Coachmakers, and all honours were paid to him when he visited Coachmakers' Hall. Sir Richard

Wallace, Bart., to whom London owes the wonderful house of artistic treasures known as the Wallace Collection, was also made an honorary freeman of the Company.

By this time the coachmaking trade was booming. The number of carriages in use in 1874 was 432,000, compared with 60,000 in 1814 – an increase of 372,000 in 60 years. "It is a matter for satisfaction," George Thrupp remarked, "that our trade contributes to the comfort, happiness and respectability of the community in general, and is also a very healthy trade for the workmen."

Certain members of the Company, notably Thrupp himself, George Hooper and George Maberly, who were all practical coachmakers, while supporting the encouragement of theoretical work by students and apprentices given by the annual competitions, believed that there was also a need for more technical and practical training of the workmen employed in the coachmaking trade. And so in 1883 they formed the Institute of British Carriage Manufacturers with a committee consisting largely of members of the Coachmakers' Company. The first President was George N. Hooper. In the years to come the two organisations were to work closely together, especially in holding competitions for designs and drawings of vehicles. The Institute usually met in Coachmakers' Hall.

George Hooper, incidentally, later became involved with an unusual aspect of coach design when he travelled to Lyons to examine the carriage in which President Carnot had been assassinated. As he suspected, the carriage was so lowhung and shallow that it gave the assassin every chance to strike with a knife or bullet. He brought back four photographs and sent a report to the French Government advising them to protect their future Presidents by giving them deeper carriages hung higher – and his warning was heeded. He also made the point that if the two footmen behind had been seated instead of standing, they would have been in a better position to protect M. Carnot. Instead, they had their work cut out to balance themselves by clinging to the shaking carriage.

The coachmaking firms in Victorian times ranged from one-man businesses making one-off carriages in small towns to companies with a large output and stock. W. & F. Thorn, for example, who were coachmakers and coach harness makers to the Queen, made four of the most fashionable carriages in London – the Square Town Sociable, the Single Brougham, the Canoe Open-Quarter Victoria, and the Skeleton Phaeton. They always had 300 vehicles in stock at their Great Portland street premises.

In the absence of complete lists of members before 1870, it is impossible to judge how many of the large number of 19th-century coachbuilders in the United Kingdom were liverymen of the Company. The proportion was certainly small. The Company had fallen to a low ebb with only 74 liverymen in 1870, even though at some stage – probably in the 1860s – entry had been widened to accept people outside the coachmaking business altogether, which was probably why the Livery increased to 105 by the end of the century. Although its jurisdiction 20 miles round London was no longer valid, the Company was still basically a London institution.

This small membership of fewer than 100 has to be compared with the 400 or more coachmakers (of whom about 100 were located in London) in the list of British coachmakers which Mrs. Watney has compiled so far from her study of old books on carriages, modern auction sale catalogues and other sources and which she has kindly made accessible to the Company. The total number of coachmakers in Britain at the end of the century can only be guessed at – some estimates put it as high as well over 1,000, many being individuals working in a very small way in towns and even villages.

Famous coachmaking names of the late 18th- and the 19th-centuries included among the past-Masters of the Company were Baxter and Pearce (the partners in that firm), Birch, Berry, Blizzard, the three partners of Collingridge, Cook and Rowley, Edwards, Glover, Hatchett, Holland, Holmes, Hooper (George and William), Hopkinson, Houlditch, Thorn and Turrill.

Lionel Lukin (Master in 1793), who was a fashionable coachmaker in Long Acre, achieved additional fame after his death as the prime inventor of the life-boat. His "unsubmergible boat" had airtight and watertight spaces at stem and stern, giving such buoyancy that the craft would hold far more than the normal burden of crew and passengers, even when they stood in water. Lukin's *Experiment* crossed the Channel several times when other boats would not face the wild weather; then some Continental smuggler stole it. Honours and awards went to others, as is the

PLATE 21
The delightful trade card of Joseph Cockshoot, advertising "Splendid Suits of Wedding Equipages – Chariots, Open Clarences, Landaus and Charabanks."

not uncommon fate of inventors, but Lukin's prior claim is now universally recognised. There is a memorial window to him at Hythe church in Kent, where he is buried.

The name of another past-Master of the late 18th-century, Henry Nash (1784), came to the notice of the Company 100 years later in a sad fashion.

George Hooper recounted the incident in a lecture he gave at the Mansion House in 1896:

> Nash's descendants fell on evil days and poverty, for not many years ago the Master Coach Builders' Benevolent Institution elected, as a pensioner, an old member of that family who told me that his ancestors had carried on their business of carriage builders in the City of London, in succession from father to son, from the reign of King Charles II to that of Queen Victoria, and that he was the last of the race. Feeling interested in such a man and his misfortunes, I asked him to write out some of the facts relating to his family and send them to me. He was much worn and feeble through the troubles he had passed through. I never had the information I asked for so, with his death, all clues to his ancestors perished.

The turn from the 18th- to the 19th-century produced a family that created a new record in having four members who became Masters of the Company. The firm of Windus carried on their business at 73 Bishopsgate Street Within, and were coachmakers to the Rothschilds. This was more important than it might seem because it was the custom of the Rothschild bankers to keep in touch personally; and with branches in all the great capitals of Europe this entailed constant travelling over long distances with speed and punctuality. The reliability of their coaches and carriages was therefore of the utmost importance, and the Windus vehicles evidently provided this to their full satisfaction. The four members of the Windus family who were Masters were Arthur (1794), Edward (1810), Thomas (1823) and Benjamin (1826). Charles Baxter, Master in 1819, was one of the great Long Acre colony of coachmakers and supplied vehicles to Queen Adelaide. Luke Hopkinson (Master in 1822) elevated coachmaking to a profession, being consulted as an adviser on his customers' special requirements and gaining a footing of personal friendship with many of them. Thomas Glover, Master in 1829, acquired particular fame as a maker of carriage springs.

No list of famous Coachmakers in the 19th-century would be complete without a special reference to the Peters family, who set up a new record in providing five Masters of the Company. Their contribution began with Thomas Peters (1846), who started the large and flourishing business of Peters & Sons, and he was followed by his three sons, John (1858), William (1860), and Joseph (1862). Col. James Peters (1863), probably Thomas's brother, had retired from the firm many years earlier. The ultimate record for the number of Masters in one family is six, and is held by the Chancellors. Three brothers, John (1839), Thomas (1840) and George (1844) were followed more than half a century later by Frederic (1878) and his two sons Albert (1901) and Capt. Frederic Chancellor (1906).

Mrs. Watney's invaluable directory, supplemented by other sources, shows that the following liverymen of the Company (in addition to the past-Masters) were among the true coachmakers of the 19th-century, the figures in brackets indicating the dates of their admission:

Frederick Stocken, Halkin Street (1845)
Frederick Glover, of Glover, Webb & Liversedge,
    London (1870)
Richard Boyall, London and Grantham (1872)
William Hewitt, Chester (1873)
John Merry, Derby (1873)
John Ridges, Wolverhampton (1873)
Charles Windover, Long Acre (1873)
Charles Thorn, Great Portland Street (1873)
James Corben, Great Queen Street (1873)
George Maberley, Oxford Street (1873)
Frederick Shanks, Great Queen Street (1873)
Charles Curtis, Long Acre (1873)
George Holmes, Margaret Street (1875)
William Silk, Long Acre (1876)
Robert Silk, Long Acre (1876)
Henry Thorn, London (1877)
Frederick Thorn, London (1877)
William Thorn, London (1877)
George Hopkinson, London (1881)
Oliver Thorn, London (1882)
Alexander Henderson, Glasgow (1893)
John Clark, Aberdeen (1893)
John Philipson, Newcastle-on-Tyne (1896)

George Maberly, who had his coach and harness making
business in Welbeck Street and Marylebone Lane, joined George
and Herbert Thrupp in Oxford Street in 1858 to become the
famous firm of Thrupp and Maberly.

Although London was regarded as the chief seat of carriage
manufacture, Edinburgh, Bristol, Derby, Dublin, Glasgow,
Liverpool, Manchester, Newcastle-on-Tyne, Nottingham and
Southampton all produced large numbers, and there were coachmakers in many small towns. Unhappily, orders from abroad for
coaches and carriages declined to the point where France and
Austria had a much bigger export trade than Great Britain. But
British skills in coachmaking were still respected, and the Imperial
carriage works at St. Petersburg were managed by an Englishman
in the 1870s.

As the 19th-century drew to a close, the progress made in

transport since the early days of the Company was summed up by John Philipson, a future-Master, in his presidential address to the Institute of British Carriage Manufacturers at Tunbridge Wells in 1895:

> Two hundred years ago, the journey from London to Tunbridge Wells was considered a formidable day's ride on horseback. Forty years afterwards, in 1735, visitors came down from London in their Post-Chaises, which occupied seven hours on the journey, while a little later, flies (one-horse hackney carriages) compassed the distance in five-and-a-half hours. Today the journey is done by rail in less than sixty minutes. It may be accomplished by road in three-and-a-half hours, thanks to McAdam and the excellent Coaches which run from Northumberland Avenue.

As we shall see in the next chapter, Philipson also looked ahead to "a reality which we, as coachmakers, will have to face in the future". Even as he spoke, the Lanchester brothers were completing the first all-British, four-wheel, petrol-driven motor car – and the days of the horse-drawn carriage were numbered.

11 Learning to live with the Motor Car

JOHN Philipson seems to have been the first coachmaker to put on record his views about the probable development of the horseless carriage. He did so in August 1895 in the speech referred to in the previous chapter, and his words are worth recalling some 80 years later:

> The fact that a Bill has recently been introduced in the House of Commons to amend the law with respect to the use of locomotives on highways is one that no coachmaker can regard with indifference. Its object is to exempt carriages, propelled by other means than horse-power, from the regulations of the Locomotives Act in cases where they are not used for traction purposes. Now, the Locomotives Act was passed mainly with the object of applying to engines used for traction purposes, and it was totally inapplicable to the light horseless carriages which are used in Paris and other parts of France. By the law of this country, the road engine cannot proceed at a greater speed than four miles per hour in the town, and the object of the new Bill is to remove the legal obstacle as to speed in order that we may try those light self-propelled carriages which are used in France, where they are very correctly called "automobiles". It is not to be believed that our country, which builds locomotives as excellent as any that are made, and which, for a long time, led the world in their production, can any longer refrain from following the lead of its neighbours in experiments which have yielded such valuable results. The opinion has recently been expressed in the *Standard* that, if once the trammels are taken off this method of locomotion in the United Kingdom, the development that will follow will assuredly grow to extraordinary proportions, and I am bound to confess that I concur in this view.

Two months after John Philipson had thus declared his faith in the future of the motor car, the Britannia Electric Carriage Syndicate, Limited, of Colchester, suggested to the Coachmakers' Company that they should add to the prizes offered annually for designs for horse-drawn carriages one or two prizes for designs of motor cars. The Clerk's reply was that as the list for the 1896 competition had been completed and recently announced, it was not practical now to offer special prizes. In fact, the vehicles for which designs and models were called for that year were Double Broughams, Sociables and Dog Carts, while the Master offered a couple of prizes for a fully coloured design in perspective of a light State carriage, without a perch, "suited for Oriental markets". This may have been prompted by the command given recently by Queen Victoria to Joseph Peters, past-Master and head of the famous coachmaking firm, to build a State Coach as a present for the Ameer of Afghanistan.

But interest in the motor car was now growing so rapidly that the Company could no longer stand aloof. In the New Year, 1896, it was announced that an International Horse and Horseless Carriage and Roads Locomotive Exhibition was to be held at the Crystal Palace in May. The Company found itself involved willy-nilly in the organisation because Sir Walter Wilkin, the Lord Mayor of London, who accepted the Presidency of the Honorary Council of Advice for the Exhibition, was also Master of the Coachmakers – the first time in the Company's history that the two appointments had been held concurrently. In March it was announced that the executive committee to deal with horse-drawn vehicles at the Exhibition included six past-Masters of the Company (Robert Alford, 1886; Charles Bartlett, 1888; Frederic Chancellor, 1878; George N. Hooper, 1874; Sir John Monckton, Town Clerk of London, 1892/93; and Col. James Peters, 1863), as well as several members (Andrew W. Barr, John Philipson, and Peter de Lande Long, the Clerk).

Although the Exhibition, which opened on Saturday 2 May 1896 in the presence of 10,000 people, consisted mostly of carriages, State coaches and other horse-drawn vehicles of historical interest (among them the original Brougham lent by the Company), it was the demonstration of horseless carriages in motion in the grounds of the Crystal Palace that attracted most attention. Only seven of the 17 motor cars arranged by the great pioneer

PLATE 22
*A carriage without a horse was a
sight to marvel at only 80 years ago.
From a painting by F. Gordon
Crosby.*

motorist, Sir David Salomans, were on parade when the Lord
Mayor and his *entourage*, including a delegation of Coachmakers,
arrived to see them show off their paces, but even the cynics and
sceptics had to admit they were impressed. *The County Gentleman*,
for example, commented:

> Sir David Saloman's Victoria, as steered by that
> gentleman, certainly left little to desire as regards speed
> and ease of handling.

The writer continued:

> An unpleasant vibration, and a pervasive odour which does not recall Araby the Blest, appear to be the principal drawbacks to these "carriages of the future". But even if the removal of these drawbacks is within the resources of science, we need not fear for our old friend the horse. Some of the most enthusiastic of the motor men have been talking as if he would soon share the fate of the Dodo and the Mastodon. Do not believe it. The horse will neither be killed by the electric spark, nor will he be drowned in rivers of oil.

Just before the Crystal Palace exhibition opened John Philipson was presented with the freedom of the Company by Sir Walter Wilkin, the Lord Mayor and Master, in recognition of 12 years' work in promoting technical education in coachmaking. His father had been a liveryman and his uncle a member of the Court. All were partners in the firm of Atkinson & Philipson, the Newcastle-on-Tyne coachmakers who had been in business since 1794. They claimed the distinction of making the earliest first class railway carriages, which they did by the simple expedient of mounting the bodies of stage coaches on trucks. In collaboration with William, his elder son, John Philipson wrote several text books including *The Art and Craft of Coachmaking; Harness; The Theory of Draught;* and *Suspension.* His younger son, also John, was to become Master in 1916.

The success of the Crystal Palace demonstration encouraged more people to urge the Company to include motor cars within the scope of the annual design competition, both the Self-Propelled Traffic Association and the London Chamber of Commerce lending their weight to the idea. In October 1896 the Company made the inevitable concession and included in the rules for next year's competition a prize for "Designs of a self-propelled light motor carriage, side elevation, half-front and half-back; two-inch scale, details of mechanism six-inch scale. Copyright to remain property of competitor."

One month later the Light (Road) Locomotive Bill became an Act of Parliament and was immediately celebrated by the famous Motor Car Tour from London to Brighton, which is commemorated in the R.A.C. Veteran Car Run every year. It was sub-titled the First Meet of the Motor Car Club – an appropriate description because the vehicles that took part were horseless carriages. The Act was to cause fundamental change in the Company as the horse-drawn carriage was challenged and eventually superseded (except as a vehicle for recreation) by the motor car.

After all the fuss beforehand the result of the 1897 competition was an anti-climax, for when it was judged at Coachmakers' Hall in May there were only two entries – and neither was considered of sufficient merit to deserve a prize. This gave enormous satisfaction to those who were opposed to the motor car. *The Pall Mall Gazette*, for example, headed its story "The Motor-Car Ostracised" and went on to report: "The competition, it may not come as a stunning surprise to the people of England to hear, was a woeful failure." And *The English Mechanic*, after recapitulating the indifferent performances of horseless carriages in various competitions and demonstrations, concluded: "No permanent trade will be done in them."

In the circumstances it was understandable, though regrettable, that the Coachmakers' Company ignored the motor car in its annual competitions for designs and models for the next five years. Their attitude towards the motor car at this time was expressed by Alexander Henderson, a member of the Livery who was an active coachmaker, in his presidential address to the Institute of British Carriage Manufacturers at Southampton in 1897:

> As Coachmakers, we should in the first place be prepared to build a carriage for any motor that may be introduced. In the meantime we build carriages for the horse as motor, and are required to produce vehicles for any sized pony or horse from the 10 hands pony to the 17 hands horse. We know that the motor carriage has been tried and experimented with on many occasions; but on every one of the many varieties some objectionable feature has been fatal to its success and adoption as a vehicle for private use. Possibly in course of time these defects may be removed and a perfectly satisfactory motor result. Yet, however perfect the motor may eventually become, in my opinion most

people will still prefer, for private use, the life-like, animated appearance of well-appointed horse traction to any dead mechanism, however smoothly it glides along. We should remain neutral, and be in a position to supply carriages for any motor that is introduced or required by a customer.

A couple of years before Henderson spoke, Atkinson & Philipson had given a lead by announcing that in future they were to be regarded as motor carriage builders and repairers as well as carriage and harness makers. They did in fact produce a few steam carriages, but they did not become regular motor manufacturers. In the following year, 1896, *The Autocar* described an electric Victoria made by Thrupp and Maberly for the Queen of Spain. It was in fact the fifth such vehicle they had made, but they did not make any more. This one was "a canoe-shaped Victoria of the neatest design, fitted with a powerful brake and ingenious steering gear". It was made under instructions from a Spanish engineer named Julian. The journal added that "the vehicle was pronounced by all of those who have inspected it to be one of the most elegant and best finished autocars yet made."

The Financial News warned that "carriage builders will have to convert themselves partially into engineers", but none of the established coachmakers moved into the new world of full-scale motor manufacture. They were content to restrict themselves to making bodies – when necessary, for vehicles without horses. (It was not until many years later that William Lawton-Goodman, a liveryman whose firm had made carriages for many years, took over the Whitlock Automobile Company, which had been founded in 1902, and tried to revive the Whitlock car, a hybrid vehicle with Lawton-Goodman coachwork. And in 1923 George Salmons, who joined the Livery in 1931, started the Salmons Light Car Company to make the NP car at his coachworks at Tickford Street, Newport Pagnell, which later became the home of the Aston Martin car.)

Meanwhile in 1898 the Company co-operated with the Institute of British Carriage Manufacturers, the Technical Education Board of the London County Council, and the governing body of the Polytechnic in founding the Polytechnic Day School of Carriage Building, which provided practical and technical education of a high order for those already in, or about to enter the trade. An outcome of these negotiations was that Quintin Hogg, founder of the Polytechnic (and the father of Lord Hailsham, who became Lord Chancellor) was made a freeman of the Company in acknowledgement of his service to technical education in the coachmaking industry. In 1894 the Company also decided to offer the freedom to Baroness Burdett-Coutts in recognition of her generous assistance in providing a technical course which attracted many students. In a modest little speech of acknowledgement and thanks, Lady Burdett-Coutts said she ventured to think that some improvement had been made in vehicles generally since she first became acquainted with the streets of London. She was born a year before Waterloo.

PLATE 23
This magnificent State Postillion Landau was built by Hoopers for King Edward VII in 1902. It is customarily used open by the Queen for meeting foreign heads of state and is drawn by six grey postillion horses. This photograph was taken during the state visit of King Olaf of Norway to Edinburgh in 1962.

At the beginning of 1900 the Company contributed £157. 10s to the equipment fund for the force of Imperial Volunteers raised by the City for the South African War. In recognition of this support the Company was collectively awarded the South African Medal. The Volunteers were given a ceremonial farewell. Each man was enrolled as a freeman of the City at Guildhall, and after a service at St. Paul's the force were entertained at supper in the Middle Temple Hall and the Lincoln's Inn Hall. The next day they sailed from Southampton.

Some months later they were followed to South Africa by a Royal Commission, who condemned the military horse-drawn ambulance in their report on the care and treatment of the

PLATE 24

For the State Opening of Parliament the Queen normally uses the Irish State Coach, seen here in 1967. The original coach, made by Thomas Hutton of Dublin, was destroyed by fire while being overhauled at Barkers' premises in 1911. The present vehicle built by Barkers is an exact replica.

wounded. The Master of the Coachmakers, Col. Stohwasser of the Honourable Artillery Company, immediately offered three prizes in the next annual competition for improved designs which would be lighter and more comfortable, and would carry more men. The competition was one of the largest and most successful for many years and the help of military experts was obtained in judging the 42 entries. The winner was a Mr. Terry of Fulham, second prize going to John Philipson.

The name of a family that was to be prominent in the Company appeared in the 1900 competition when John O. H. Norris of Cockshoots, the famous firm of Manchester coachmakers, won the bronze medal and £3 for the best working drawing of a double Brougham; he also headed the list in the competition for drawings of a Governess Cart and a T-Cart. John Norris was the brother of Sydney Norris, Master in 1931, and his son, Graham, was to become Master in turn.

But the Company was not allowed to forget about motor cars. On 29 April 1901 *The Times* remarked:

> To judge by what is seen in the public streets, many manufacturers of motor cars seem to vie with each other in regard to ugliness rather than grace. It might therefore be of advantage if the Coachmakers' Company would include motor cars in their next competition and offer prizes to encourage elegance of design in those vehicles.

For another year the Company held out. Then at a dinner at the Grocers' Hall in July 1902 the Master, Albert Chancellor (an auctioneer and estate agent) said:

> The Company have been asked to look into the motor business. When we do, we hope we will get something that will make a little less dust, and cause less unpleasant odours, than now prevail.

In October the rules for the 1903 competition were announced, including the design for:

> A motor car body to carry four people in the hind

part and one or two on the driver's seat, suitable for a petrol engine. The hind part to be convertible from an open to a closed carriage.

No details of the machinery were required beyond what would be visible in the drawing. *The Field* commented: "Carriage builders who were apt to resent the advent of the motor car are becoming resigned to the inevitable." The winning design was submitted by A. Boag, an apprentice aged 18. Thenceforth there was a motor car class in the competition every year – in 1907 the subject was "a small light motor car body to suit two persons, suitable for a country practitioner." The Company also made an annual contribution to the prize fund for coachwork competitions organised by the City and Guilds of London Institute.

The Coachmakers' Company was busily working at preparations to welcome the Chambre Syndicate des Carrossiers of Paris on their visit to London in September, 1909, when a world event occurred – the English Channel was flown! It is not easy after the lapse of years to convey in words the enthusiasm which the flight occasioned. Some of the excitement spread to the Company, which on Election Day sent the following resolution to M. Blériot:

> That the Court of the Coachmakers' and Coach Harness Makers' Company, which is closely identified with the motor industry, desires to convey its hearty congratulations to M. Blériot on his recent successful flight of the Channel, this being the first meeting of the Court since its achievement.

The Company, it will be noticed, did not yet envisage the aeroplane as a matter of trade concern, except that it used a petrol engine. Two years later the Institute of Belgo–Dutch carriage builders were in London, and again the Master received at Coachmakers' Hall, where an exhibition of the Company's possessions was staged.

The neutral attitude towards the motor car, advocated by Henderson and adopted widely by the trade, was fostered by the way in which the manufacture of motor cars developed. Coachmakers were not equipped to make complete motor cars, knowing nothing about engines and transmissions; and most of the motor

PLATE 25
The early motor cars had "carriage" bodies, as seen in this Siddeley landaulette with Hooper coachwork supplied to King Edward VII.

manufacturers did not need their help in the supply of bodies – they made them in their own factories. As more and more motor cars took to the roads in place of horse-drawn vehicles, the number of coachmakers up and down the country grew smaller and smaller. The few that survived were those who took advantage of the fact that the motor car of those days was built as a chassis on which the body was mounted separately. They accordingly offered special bodies which could be ordered by motorists who demanded an individual character in their motor cars. There was also scope for supplying bodies to motor manufacturers who did not possess their own coachworks. Hoopers, for example, received an order from Wolseley in 1907 for 20 motor car bodies – at a cost of £4,557 for the lot. At the Motor Show at Olympia two years earlier the coachmakers W. & F. Thorn (both partners were liverymen) displayed a convertible body "to suit any chassis", the conversion being from a Landaulette with a hard-top passenger compartment to an open Victoria with a folding hood. In both cases the driver sat in the open.

126

On the stand of Mulliners of Northampton was shown a three-seated Landaulette on a Napier chassis which *The Autocar* described as the most original example of body building in the exhibition. The journal explained . . . .

> . . . . hitherto when a Landaulette has been used for conveying two ladies and a gentleman to theatres, dinners, etc., it has been necessary for the male passenger to travel on the outside seat beside the driver, or to be cramped within, uncomfortably seated on a child's inconvenient seat. To overcome this objection Mr. Mulliner has built a very handsome and tasteful body in which the seat hitherto occupied by the left-hand front seat is built into the body of the Landaulette itself, and becomes part and parcel of the interior. The driver remained outside in the cold.

Alford & Alder offered "Laminated wood motor bodies in any shape" (with aluminium or steel panels if desired) and exhibited specimens on the Singer and Clement-Talbot stands. The history of this firm went back to the early part of the 19th-century when Thomas Alford, who was trained as a cabinet maker, set up as a coachmaker at 9, King's Row, Newington Butts, South London. As such he was listed in the Post Office directory of 1824; he died while still a young man six years later. The business was carried on by his widow until his son was old enough to take over. In the 1860s Robert Alford asked his foreman, Thomas Packwood Alder, to join him in partnership as Alford & Alder. In due course of time they became Masters of the Coachmakers' Company in successive years. Robert Greenwood Alford, Robert's son, went into accountancy but became Master of the Company in 1907. Vincent, his son, continued the business which grew into a large engineering company, and became Master in turn in 1940. By 1910 Alford & Alder were making motor car bodies of all kinds from taxicabs to landaulettes, and were sending them as far afield as Australia and South Africa. In *The Motor* they advertised a:

> Light Landaulette Body, with Canopy, Patent "Fastlock" Wind Screen, Luggage Rail, Upholstered

either Cord Cloth or Leather, Speaking Tube, Electric
Light Fittings to Roof, to carry 4 persons inside £135,
including Mudguards, Steps and Painting Chassis.

A Torpedo body, with Torpedo Shield in front, cost £90.

Meanwhile many of the old coachmaking firms gave up the
struggle and either went out of business entirely or were taken
over by others who were adapting themselves to the new conditions. Thrupp and Maberly, for example, absorbed Edwards,
Son & Chamberlayne (George Edwards had been Master of the
Coachmakers in 1898), Keens, Holmes Brothers, and Rogers.
They did not stop there, and in 1912 they acquired the premises
and goodwill of one of the most historic coachmakers, Holland
and Holland (not to be confused with the famous gunsmiths of
the same name), who for many years had made most of the
vehicles for the Four-in-Hand and Coaching Clubs. With
Holland went their two associates, Wyburn & Company and Silk
and Sons.

Lt.-Col. Arthur F. Mulliner, one of the famous coachmaking family, was Master when the annual Livery Dinner was
held in 1910 in the presence of the Lord Mayor and "a great
number of motorists", including Mr. Edward Manville, President
of the Society of Motor Manufacturers and Traders. Manville
(afterwards Sir Edward) was chairman of the Daimler Company
and became Master in 1929. He was admitted to the Livery in
1911, the same year as John Siddeley, who had started the
Siddeley Autocar Company in Coventry in 1902 and was in the
process of forming the Siddeley–Deasy Company. These two
can therefore be considered the first of the new breed of coachmakers, the motor manufacturers, for whom the Coachmakers
was to become the natural livery company. John Siddeley's
admission was the beginning of a splendid family association with
the Company. He himself was elected Master in 1933 – and was
created Baron Kenilworth four years later. His son Cyril, Col.
Lord Kenilworth, became Master in turn in 1956 and his grandson, John Siddeley, the third Lord Kenilworth, completed the
hat-trick by becoming Master in 1969.

Manville and Siddeley were joined in the Livery in 1913 by
Herbert Austin, who had built one of the first cars in Britain,
the Wolseley three-wheeler, in 1895 – Austin did not make cars

under his own name until 1906. (In 1918 he was knighted and was elected as Assistant of the Court in the same year. He eventually became Master in 1934, and two years later was created Baron Austin of Longbridge).

What did ordinary people think of the change from horse-drawn to horse-less carriages, and what were their impressions of the motor car? Here is a fanciful account of two young ladies being given their first ride, as described by Rebecca West in her novel *The Fountain Overflows*, published by Macmillan & Company Limited.

"Claribel and Anna Matilda will be as pleased as punch, going home in a motor car won't they? What'll the family say, seeing the two come home in a real live motor car? Why, look the mere thought of it has set 'em grinning like a couple of cats with a saucer of cream, though they're much prettier, being young ladies."

Here he was quite right. We were intoxicated past speech by the idea of going home, or going anywhere, in a motor car. Some months before, Papa, in the course of a visit to a Scottish peer who admired his political writings, had been driven from and to the station in such a vehicle; but he did such things, he had crossed the Andes on a mule, and had rounded the Cape of Good Hope four times. We had never hoped to rival our father in that sphere. We knew that motor cars were the way people would travel in the future, but that brought us no nearer them, for as they grew more common we became more poor, and they were fabulously expensive. We knew that, for Mamma had read out of the paper that one cost £1,020 and she said it seemed shameful when there was no opera in England outside London and little enough inside it.

Then Mr. Phillips came in with George. The two men had both put on huge coats and caps with deep peaks and earflaps, and Mr. Phillips made his wife go and fetch rugs and shawls to wrap round us .... Aunt Lily came out of the drawing room to help the servants bring in the lemonade that you get at a party when it is time for you to go home, and found us in the hall, waiting till the motor car stopped at the gate, because Mr. Phillips and George said they did not want us to get in till they had brought it out of the coach-house, because the fumes in there were always rather horrid.

Of course it was interesting to drive in a motor-car. The miracle of not being pulled by anything, of the nothingness in front of the driver, was more staggering than can now be believed, partly because it would seem impossible that people so long accustomed to trains should have been so startled by the motor car. But a locomotive closely resembles an animal in its ardour and its breathy moodiness, and anyway it was there, in front of the carriage you sat in, pulling a weight, according to a principle grasped not only by the mind but also by the muscles. But to sit in anything which moved along by some impulse within itself, which seemed to have nothing to do with the lever and the fulcrum, was an experience which neither brain nor the arms nor the legs could understand.

Rosamund and I sat in a bewildered ecstasy which continued unabated for some time, surviving several discouragements. For there was no windscreen and we were blown about as if we stood on an Atlantic headland. There was also a pestilential atmosphere, far worse than now seems credible on the mechanical facts. I cannot think why the interior of this motor car, winnowed by the gale of its passage, should have been as murky and evil-smelling as a tunnel in the old Underground. Though Rosamund and I were very happy we felt very sick, partly because of the fumes, and partly because of our violent and irregular progress. The car went ahead quickly and passionately for a hundred or two hundred yards at a time, then halted with a spine-jerking crash, and either started again or ran backwards for some yards and stopped in a paroxysm of asthma, till George, crying to Mr. Phillips, "Don't you touch nothing," got us going again.

Three times we stopped dead. The first found us in Lovegrove High Street, and we were immediately surrounded by a crowd of youths, who put their heads inside the car and insincerely pretended that we were in a position to sell them roasted chestnuts. George got down and struck something with a hammer . . . . He jerked us on through the sea of mocking faces, and the suffocating smell began again.

Then at the corner of a crescent, about ten minutes from our home, we began to reverse, working up to a considerable speed, emitting puffs of smoke. George had some trouble in coming to a stop, and got out with the hammer, saying, "I want no help". He never once called Mr. Phillips "sir". We sat still and tried to look calm, and we debated in whispers whether it would be rude to ask Mr. Phillips whether the car was actually on fire. At this point the smoke that was puffing out of the front of the car changed its rhythm. This left us still uncertain whether the car was on fire or not, and though we were not really frightened, we were feeling in the darkness for the door handle so that we could jump if the worst came to the worst, when George leaped back into the driver's seat, just in time to take the wheel before we rushed off on the longest continuous run of the journey. For more than five minutes we proceeded in the same direction, without reversing once, and at such a pace that people on the pavements stopped dead to look at us with expressions of alarm that Rosamund and I commented on as indicating cowardice and lack of enterprise but which we feared most prophetic good sense. Then the car, after bumping the kerb, stopped with suddenness which jolted us both off our seats, and began to emit smoke not in puffs but in a continuous stifling cloud.

We were now not more than three minutes from home; we were in the main street, from which Love-grove Place turned off. But was it as rude to get out of a motor car because it had broken down as it would be to walk out of a party because the servants were late in bringing the tea? We did not know what the etiquette was, but Rosamund said, "You know, they will be anxious". So I pulled down the window and timidly called Mr. Phillips by his name.

He was within a foot of me, and for the moment had come to a halt. But he did not hear me. So I leaned out of the window and called down to him, "Mr. Phillips, we are quite close to our home, we think our mammas will be getting anxious, would you mind if we got out and walked home?" But he neither heard nor saw me. He was contemplating some fact which had turned him to stone.

Mr. Phillips turned about and got in beside us, saying "It's all right, George always finds what's wrong. Splendid fellow, George, you mustn't mind what he says." Then we sped forward, and with a great lurch at the corner, we found ourselves in Lovegrove Place, and we were again intoxicated with pride in our adventure and the nonchalance with which we had embarked on it, and we were glad because the motor car at that point developed a new and peculiar noise, like a kettledrum being played very slowly. Everybody would come running out to see what was happening, and they would be astonished when they discovered that it was us.

But nobody came out."

12 The New Coachmakers*

ON the outbreak of war in 1914 the Livery numbered 102, three less than it had been at the beginning of the century. All festivities came to an end, but the design competitions were held in 1915 when a prize was offered for a horse-drawn ambulance body, with improved stretchers. After that, the competitions were suspended for the duration of the war and were not revived until 1924.

The annual Livery dinner was cancelled in 1914 and (with the single exception of 1919) was not resumed till 1927, when Prince Arthur of Connaught was the guest.

Prince Arthur accepted the freedom and livery of the Company in May 1927 and was afterwards elected an Assistant. He continued to show interest in the Company and was made Master in 1932. To commemorate his admission Arthur Hungerford Pollen, who was Master in 1927, gave a Prince Arthur Golf Cup. This is a silver-gilt trophy which is competed for annually by the Livery Companies of London in a foursomes tournament organised by the Coachmakers' Company at various courses in the Home Counties. Each Company is represented by two pairs. The first competition was held at Walton Heath in 1927. The Prince Arthur Cup has been one of the most successful functions of the Coachmakers' Company and in 1976 it brought together 47 Livery Companies at Wentworth, which is now its home.

The coachmakers who had adapted themselves to the change from the horse-drawn carriage to the motor car in the Edwardian era enjoyed what was to be a final period of glory in the 1920s and 1930s. The companies bearing such famous names as Hooper, Barker, Windover, Thrupp and Maberly, Rippon, Cockshoot, the Mulliners (there were three separate concerns), Vincent, Harrington, Offord and Arnold – all in this list being represented in the Livery – created motor car bodies of great luxury. A newcomer, Park Ward, was started in 1919 by William McDonald Park, who became Master in 1949, and Charles William Ward (whose son, also Charles William, was to be elected Master in 1975, but tragically died during his term of office).

*See Introduction.

133

The decline of the individual wood-framed, steel (for aluminium) panelled coachbuilt body started in the 1930s when the advantages of independent front suspension in comfort and handling were discovered. To work properly, the suspension had to be attached to a completely rigid unit, and so the separate chassis, on which a variety of special bodies could be mounted, was largely replaced by a combined all-steel chassis/body structure to which the engine and running gear were attached. Up to 1939 all Rolls-Royces and Bentleys, as well as some other large cars, continued to be supplied as a chassis, so there was still scope for coachmakers to carry on their trade, but in 1946, when the Crewe factory resumed motor car production, a "standard" Bentley model was introduced with a pressed steel, integral construction body of uniform design supplied by the Pressed Steel Company of Oxford. Three years later the same treatment was given to the

PLATE 26
The best of both worlds! A 40 horse-power Lanchester with chassis lengthened to accommodate a special carriage body – something between a double landau and a brougham – built by Lanchester themselves in 1924 for the Maharajah of Alwar. The result was a unique hybrid.

Rolls-Royce Silver Dawn, though the Silver Wraith was still a coachbuilt saloon. But the market for independent coachmaking firms was doomed.

Some of them found refuge under the wings of large motor manufacturers, operating as coachbuilding subsidiaries; others gave up coachmaking altogether and became engineering firms or motor distributors, agents and repairers. Thrupp and Maberly had already shown the way when they joined Rootes Motors in 1925. They continued to make luxurious bodies for large cars, but after the Second World War they confined themselves to making quality bodies for some Rootes Group cars. This went on until the 1960s when Rootes closed them down. Hooper, who had absorbed their old rivals Barker in 1937, were bought up by the BSA/Daimler group after the war and made bodies for Daimler chassis until BSA sold their Daimler interest to Jaguar. That was the end of Hooper/Barker – and of a London landmark, the Hooper showroom in St. James's Street. In 1939 Park Ward were taken over by Rolls-Royce as their coach building subsidiary, in which they were joined 20 years later by H. J. Mulliner. Arthur Mulliner of Northampton gave up coachmaking during the war, while the third Mulliner concern, Mulliners of Birmingham, became the Forward Radiator subsidiary company of Leyland Cars. Cockshoot also gave up coach building and eventually became a part of the Lex chain of motor agents and repairers. Rippon followed a similar course when they joined the great Appleyard Group. Alford & Alder, one of the first of the original coachmakers to make bodies for motor cars, had turned to engineering after the 1914–18 war and later became a component manufacturing subsidiary of Leyland Cars. Lawton–Goodman turned to making commercial vehicle bodies and mobile shops.

And so the great names of coachmaking disappeared one by one, leaving only H. J. Mulliner and Park Ward to carry on the tradition, entirely for the benefit of Rolls-Royce and, of course, employing modern methods.

In spite of the rapid development of the motor industry after the First World War, there was a dearth of new members joining the Company, only one or two being enrolled each year up to 1925. The number rose to eight in 1927, dropping to two in 1930. Among those from the motor industry were Sir William Letts

(Crossley), a future Master; Fred Bennett, pioneer importer of Cadillacs (to become Master in 1950); Sidney Straker of Straker–Squire and two active coachmakers, Horace Nutt of Barkers and William Park of Park Ward.

In 1927 the Company formally recognised the manufacture of motor cars as a legitimate form of "coachmaking" by passing a resolution which provided that every alternate vacancy on the Court of Assistants would be filled by some person connected with the motor industry. And so we find Sir John Siddeley and Sir Herbert Austin being elected to the Court in 1928. The admission of Frederick Handley Page to the Livery in 1929 was much more significant than it seemed at the time, for it was to open up the Company's membership to another branch of "coachmaking", the manufacture of aircraft.

In 1931 the motor manufacturers, their agents and the remaining coachmaking firms started to show more interest in the Livery and the intake of new members rose to 19. The prime mover was William Lawton-Goodman. He had succeeded Sir Edward Manville as Master in September 1930 and was one of the old school, living above the Slade Works of his long established coachmaking company at the Broadway, Cricklewood.

The coachmakers who joined in 1931 included W. J. and H. E. R. Vincent, Col. Reginald Rippon, George Salmons and Roger Thrupp, while recruits from the motor manufacturers were Rowland (later Sir Rowland) Smith of Ford and William Bullock of Singer. Two makers of commercial vehicle bodies, Walter Bonallack and Percy Caffyn, also joined the Livery.

In his efforts to enlist new members from the motor industry Lawton-Goodman found powerful allies in the Connolly family. The father, Samuel, who joined the Livery in 1909, had founded the family currier business with a brother in the 1870s, supplying leather for saddlery and harness and then carriage upholstery and hoods. He was made an Assistant in 1928 and his three sons were admitted to the Livery in the 1930s; Edward and Wilfrid, who were to become Masters in 1952 and 1954 respectively, and Fred, who was on particularly close terms with the leading figures of the motor industry. It was sad that the three Connolly brothers died within the space of a year shortly before the Tercentenary of the Company, but in the meantime the family link with the Coachmakers had been assured by the admission of Wilfrid's sons,

Nicholas and Timothy, to the Livery in 1955.

Harness making was also represented in the Company by Samuel Withers, who joined in 1910. The brothers Samuel and Charles Withers of Shrewsbury were also well-known as coachmakers. The Company had a famous saddler as Master in 1912 – Major William Wilton, whose firm later became Champion and Wilton. Major Wilton was actually Master of the Saddlers Company when he died in 1958.

The old established coachmaking families continued to provide new members. In 1938 Graham Norris, who had been apprenticed to the Company by his father, John Norris, was elected to the Livery (becoming Master in 1961), and so too was Peter Croall, whose father, Peter Croall, J.P., was Master in that year. The Croall family of Edinburgh were proud of having been in road transport for eight reigns, having been appointed Royal Warrant holders to Queen Victoria in 1843 as Job Masters and Post Masters. In recent years they became part of the London coachmakers, H. J. Mulliner. Peter Croall, Junior, was to follow in his father's footsteps and become Master in 1962.

With the motor and aircraft industries firmly entrenched in the Company, it was only natural that the big petroleum companies should also be represented. This began in 1932 when Martin Davy of British Petroleum and G. N. Wilson of Shell Mex-BP were elected to the Livery. In both cases the Minute Book gave their company names and addresses, a departure from the usual practise and one which was to occur occasionally thereafter. The normal custom is to give the private address and, since members are not required to fill in an application form, this has been the extent of the Company's information about them. The only register is that published in the Year Book and from this it is impossible to analyse the membership. However, 1977 will see the introduction of a Who's Who section in the Year Book.

During the years between the First and Second World Wars another element entered into the Company's membership in the form of the technical press covering the motor and aircraft industries. The movement had begun in 1925 with the election of Sir Edward Iliffe, head of the family publishing company, Iliffe and Sons, among whose magazines were *The Autocar* and *Flight*. He was followed in 1931 by Roland Dangerfield, head of the rival publishers, Temple Press, who published

The Motor and The Aeroplane. Thus both catered for the industries from which the "new coachmakers" were to be drawn. Both men became Masters in due course, Iliffe in 1936 and Dangerfield in 1953. In 1933 Sir Edward Iliffe was created a Baron – the first time a serving member of the Court had been made a peer. Two years after his Mastership, Lord Iliffe presented the Company with its own History★. This was written by Walter G. Bell from material supplied and minutes and records indicated by John C. Mitchell, who had been Master in 1935. (Mitchell was Secretary of the London General Omnibus Company). The history was edited by a committee appointed by the Court and

PLATE 27
Sir Frederick Handley Page (right) *and Sir Richard Fairey.* "HP" *became Master in 1943 and brought in many new members from the aircraft industry.*

★*See* Introduction.

consisting of Capt. Frederic Chancellor, John Mitchell and Vincent Alford. In 1937, Lord Iliffe sponsored the election of Geoffrey Smith, his chief editorial executive whose son, Wing Cmdr. Maurice Smith, D.F.C., is the Master of the Coachmakers' Company in 1977, its Tercentenary Year.

After the upsurge of 1931 new membership tailed off somewhat; in 1935 there were only two enrolments. The membership of the Livery in 1939 stood at 132, compared with 97 in 1920. There were some important individual additions from the motor industry: Oliver Boden, Victor Riley and Herman Aron in 1933, Cyril Siddeley, George Beharrell and William Rootes in 1934, Charles Reeve in 1935, Capt. Arthur Waite in 1936, Miles Thomas in 1937, Harold Arthur Guy in 1938 and Leonard Lord in 1939.

In the Second World War the Company cancelled the annual Livery dinner, publication of the Year Book and the Prince Arthur Cup golf tournament. The overriding effect of the war, of course, was the destruction of the Company's Hall described earlier.

With the election of the aircraft pioneer Sir Frederick Handley Page as Master in 1943, the Company rose like a phoenix from the ashes of Noble Street. His message to the Court dispelled the gloom of war. Having considered the finances of the Company and realising that its income was now confied to the fees paid by joining members, he believed that more should be invited to join, especially from the aircraft industry. To this end he proposed that a special committee be formed to consider how to put this plan into effect. The committee consisted of "HP" himself in the chair, together with Sir William Letts, Fred Bennett, Edward Connolly and Roland Dangerfield.

The result was electrifying – 31 new members joined in 1944, including such impressive figures as Col. W. C. Devereux, Roy Dobson, Reginald Verdon-Smith, Sir George Nelson, Frederick G. Miles, George Dowty and Robert Blackburn. From the motor industry came Sir Charles Bartlett, Alfred Owen and Hubert Starley.

In the following year, 1945, Letts was Master and he showed that the pace set by Handley Page could be sustained. By the time peace returned during 1945, the Company had 184 members. The impetus continued in the post-war years and by 1950 the figure had reached 265. It was not long before the Livery

numbered 300 and there was a suggestion – not taken up – that a maximum should be imposed.

When life returned to something like normal after the war, the Court decided to supplement the annual Livery dinner at the Mansion House by three Court and Livery dinners during the year. It was also decided to celebrate the end of the war by electing two new Honorary Freemen – Marshal of the Royal Air Force Viscount Trenchard and Admiral Sir John Cunningham, Royal Navy. They were followed in later years by Lord Brabazon of Tara (1952), Field Marshal Earl Alexander of Tunis (1954) and Marshal of the Royal Air Force Sir John Slessor (1956).

PLATE 28

The restoration and maintenance of carriages and coaches has been carried on superbly by Gordon J. Offord, a descendant of the coach-making firm of that name which was founded in 1791 and continued until 1968. This semi-State coach has been immaculately restored in recent years for the Duke of Westminster's estates.

Meanwhile an Appendix to the *History* of the Company which Lord Iliffe had presented in 1938 was written by past-Master Clifford Edgar in 1950. This recorded subsequent events from 1938 on, including the loss of the Hall. Edgar was an enthusiastic member of the Madrigal Society and when he was Master in 1948 he introduced the accompaniment of madrigal singing at the Livery dinners. There is no longer any singing of madrigals, but Miss Miranda Corner, Secretary to the Clerk, sang the *Grace Laudi Spirituali* (A.D. 1545) at the Mansion House dinners in 1975 and 1976.

A pleasant little ceremony took place in 1957 when a replica of the Queen's Medal for the South African War – awarded to the Company in 1900 for its help in equipping the Imperial Volunteers – was presented to the Master at the War Office by the Secretary of State for War to replace the original medal which had been lost in the destruction of Coachmakers' Hall.

Since the loss of the Hall, the Company had been without any treasures in the way of pictures and books, but in 1963 the first step to make good this deficiency was taken. A set of exquisite coloured scale drawings of various types of carriages and other sketches was acquired. Many of them had little hinged flaps to illustrate alternative seating arrangements and other details. The drawings, by J. Gilfoy, were of carriages made by Edward, Son & Chamberlayne of 21, Newman Street, London. At the same time a copy of Felton's *A Treatise on Carriages* (1794) was presented to the Livery by J. O. H. Norris shortly before his death. After the Standing Committee had considered what to do with the drawings, they were made up into a handsome volume, complete with case. In 1969 Graham Norris drew attention to a collection of books, pictures and scrap books in the care of his father which were the property of the Company, to whom they had been presented many years ago by George Hooper and G. H. Thrupp. Charles Ward was asked to find a suitable home for them and did so, consigning them to the care of the National Motor Museum and Library at Beaulieu.

When Sir Frederick Handley Page died in May 1962, the Court decided "it would not be proper merely to note his death; his unique position in the aircraft industry and his contribution demanded more." A resolution was therefore written in the Minutes and communicated to his relatives stating that:

PLATE 29
The Coachmakers' Award to Industry Trophy. (See *page 147.*)

The Company have lost a past-Master whose intimate knowledge of the Company and its traditions were equalled by his loyal interest in it and the unflagging zest for its advancement. The Masters, Wardens and Assistants have lost a friend whose shrewd wisdom and pungent wit guided and enlivened the proceedings of every Court.

PLATE 30
The Coachmakers' Award to Industry Gold Medal.

As we have seen, the contribution of "HP" to the Company was as an individual Master.

On the other hand the Coachmakers have always been lucky in having families in the Livery who provide a continuing source of candidates for the highest office. In 1963 Lt.-Col. Richard Harris was the second member of his family to be Master, following his father Capt. Douglas Harris, who had

been Master in 1941. In 1968 Richard's brother, Col. George Harris, O.B.E., became the third member of the Harris family to be Master of the Coachmakers. Today, Richard Harris' son is apprenticed to the Company, representing another generation.

In 1964, for the second time in its existence, the Company had the distinction of its Master being simultaneously the Lord Mayor of London*. The Master in 1964 was Alderman Sir James Miller, G.B.E., who had been Lord Provost of Edinburgh in 1951–54. Although his own career had been in building and civil engineering, Sir James chose the motor car industry as the theme

PLATE 31

The first presentation of the Coachmakers' Award to Industry: (left to right) *Sir George Edwards Commander Kenneth Sellar, D.F.C (acting Master) and Sir William Lyons.*

*The previous occasion was in 1896. Sir Walter Wilkin held both offices.

for the annual Lord Mayor's Show in recognition of his position as Master of the Coachmakers' Company. The pageant was therefore arranged under its auspices.

Within the Company, the organisation was entrusted to Hubert Starley, the Renter Warden, who had learnt what was required for such occasions when he organised the cavalcades of vehicles in the Motor Industry Golden Jubilee celebrations in 1946. As Pageant Master he obtained the full support of the Society of Motor Manufacturers and Traders, who provided the services of one of their executives as organising secretary.

The 1964 Lord Mayor's Show was given an exciting start. Just before the pageant set off from Gresham Street a group of racing and rally cars made a *tour d'honneur* round part of the route and gave many spectators their first sight and sound of Lotus, Cooper, BRM and Brabham Formula I racing cars. Driving them were equally famous racing drivers, Jim Clark, Graham Hill, Bruce McLaren, Jackie Stewart and Jack Brabham. They returned in time to be loaded onto floats and take part in the pageant on its long journey to Aldwych and back.

The pageant was split into two sections, "Parade of the Past" and "Motor Show on Wheels". The pageant was led by the yellow semi-State chariot built for the first Marquess of Bath by Barkers of London in 1750. Other splendid examples of the work of great Coachmakers were to be seen among the vehicles at the end of the pageant – a blue chariot built by Hooper; a green and black chariot made by Thrupp and Maberly with the arms of the City on both panels; and a maroon semi-State coach built by Peters and Son, whose business had been incorporated in the 1930s by Offord and Sons. And, of course, there was the Lord Mayor's State Coach itself. This was built in 1757 by Joseph Berry, Master of the Company in 1749. Among the carriages towards the end of the procession was one carrying representatives of the Company of Coachmakers and Coach Harness Makers, for whom it was a memorable day.

Two years later, in 1966, when Hubert Starley was elected Master, the Court invited the City of Coventry to be the Company's guests at Mercers' Hall. Starley was a member of the fourth generation of the family since James Starley earned for himself the title of "the father of the cycle industry" in the 1870's.

After 300 years of existence, the Company – like most City Livery companies – had long since departed from its original purpose. The trade carried on in 1677 had virtually disappeared and its members now represented a wide variety of interests – industrial, professional and the Services. A link with coachmaking was still maintained, through the support given to the competitions organised annually by the Institute of British Carriage and Motor Manufacturers; and through annual gifts for the encouragement of technical progress made to the City and Guilds

PLATE 32
A reciprocal gesture. The 10″ model of the Pegasus engine used in the Harrier aircraft, presented to the Company by Rolls-Royce (Bristol Division) in recognition of the Coachmakers' Award to Industry being won by the Harrier in 1974.

of London Institute. In 1963 a research fellowship to the value of £600 a year at the College of Aeronautics at Cranfield was approved by the Court.

But something more dynamic was needed, so in 1964 the Standing Committee considered various ways of starting activities which would be suitable to the Company – and at the same time improving communications between the Court and the Livery, which many members thought were inadequate.

A long period of discussion and deliberation ensued. This culminated in the setting up of the Livery Committee in 1970 "to advance new ideas which might be forthcoming from members which would be of benefit to the Livery as a whole."

The first action of the Livery Committee was to organise a "working" dinner of liverymen at the Savile Club. From this dinner there emerged the idea of the Coachmakers' Awards to Industry, which was accepted by the Court. There were to be two awards annually, for aerospace and for motoring, the citation being "for outstanding contributions to technological advancement in transport also involving elegance and commercial significance." Silver trophies and gold medals were commissioned from Herr en Mevroux Leo de Vroomen, who designed and produced them.

These awards were made for the first time in 1972. The winners were Aerospatiale and the British Aircraft Corporation for the Anglo–French Concorde supersonic transport aircraft and Sir William Lyons for the creation of Jaguar Cars. Each of them, in their own way, illustrated the almost unbelievable progress that had been made in their respective fields. It was only 60 years since the Company had sent its congratulations to Blériot for his flight across the Channel; and only 77 years since Herbert Austin had made the Wolseley three-wheel car in 1895. Sir George Edwards for BAC and Sir William Lyons (himself a liveryman) accepted the awards at a luncheon at the Armourers' and Brasiers' Hall. The medal for the Aerospatiale share in Concorde was presented to Gen. Ziegler at the Mansion House dinner in June 1973.

Only one award was made in 1973. This was presented to Sir George Dowty (who had been Master in 1970) for his firm's development of the aircraft undercarriage over the years and for his management of the Dowty Group companies generally.

In 1974 the awards went to British Rail for the Advanced Passenger Train and to Hawker-Siddeley Aviation jointly with Rolls-Royce for the Harrier vertical take-off and landing aircraft. The awards were presented at the Mansion House dinner on 28th May to Dr. Sydney Jones of British Rail for the APT and to Mr. Ralph Hooper of Hawker-Siddeley and Sir Stanley Hooker of Rolls-Royce for the Harrier.

A party of Coachmakers was invited by British Rail, in April 1976, to inspect and ride in the Advanced Passenger Train at Old Dalby, on the disused section of line near Melton Mowbray where it had been tested. The experimental train, with its team of technicians in one of the three cars monitoring every detail of its performance, was making its last run before the lessons learnt

PLATE 33
Maurice Smith, D.F.C (right), and Professor Alan Wickens, British Rail's Director of Laboratories, pose in front of the Advanced Passenger Train with the Coachmakers' Award to Industry during a visit to the APT test track in April 1976.

during the three years of development were incorporated into prototype trains. The members of the Livery were able to monitor the train's speed and see the view of the track ahead as seen by the driver, on closed circuit television. This was all the more impressive because the APT has the unique advantage of being able to tilt the bodies of its carriages on curves, which therefore can be taken much faster than with conventional trains. On this occasion the highest speed reached was 132 m.p.h., though the APT has actually gone as fast as 152 m.p.h. The lack of noise and the smoothness at these speeds, despite an indifferent stretch of track, was most remarkable.

Whatever new activites the Livery Committee might suggest, the mainstay of the Company's life would continue to be the Livery dinners. By the judicious choice of guests, the Coachmakers' dinners have attained a prestige and influence that does great credit to the Company. For example, the Court and Livery dinner held in March 1976, at the Law Society, provided a valuable meeting with the leading figures in the aircraft industry on the eve of its nationalisation by the Government. The guests included Lord Beswick, the Chairman-designate of the new corporation, Sir Edouard Grundy, President of the Society of British Aerospace Constructors, Sir Peter Fletcher of Hawker-Siddeley and Mr. G. R. Jefferson of the British Aircraft Corporation. The Junior Warden, Eric Beverley, in proposing the toast of the guests, gave a notable contribution from the standpoint of an aircraft industry executive.

The Company's link with the motor industry was similarly consolidated at the first Court and Livery dinner over which the current Master, Wing-Commander Maurice Smith, D.F.C., presided at the Barber-Surgeons' Hall in November 1976. The guests included David Plastow, president of the Society of Motor Manufacturers & Traders and managing director of Rolls-Royce Motors, Lord Stokes, president of Leyland Cars, Sir Clive Bossom, chairman of the Royal Automobile Club, and the Hon. Gerald Lascelles, president of the British Racing Drivers' Club.

This was the dining tradition of the Coachmakers' Company at its 20th-century best.

Long may it continue!

13 The Company Dines

THE Coachmakers' and Coach Harness Makers' Company has continued to dine ever since that day which witnessed its incorporation in 1677, and without doubt the leading spirits in the trade met at the table long before that. Liverymen had good reason for dining together. Among the Companies of London in those days the duties of the Master, Wardens and Assistants were so often disciplinary; the Livery dinner gave the required occasion for their appearance in a more genial capacity.

One gains respect for the liverymen of days past when considering the menus of substantial dishes, and the number of them, which were placed upon the board at the Company's feasts. Here, for example, is what was provided on a Lord Mayor's Day when William III ruled England. For breakfast, it will be noted, the old coachmakers merely toyed with the fare – a couple of sirloins sufficed – but the dinner was a man's business:

5 Oct. 1697 – For breakfast:
5 soopes   2 surloins of beefe
For Dinner
5 messe of pulletts, Bacon & oysters, 3 in a dish
5 surloins of Beefe
5 Lumber Pyes
5 meese of geese, 2 in a dish
5 messe of Tongs (tongues) & udders, 2 in a dish
5 messe of custards
5 messe of capons, 3 in a dish
5 messe of fruite
5 messe of Tarts
5 messe of wild fowle

The "lumber pies" were usually found on the bill of fare; these were savoury pies made of meat or fish with eggs. The passion for udders continued for years, but a more elegant repast was ordered in the reign of Queen Anne:

1 Sep. 1704 That the Bill of fare for dinner on Eleccon day shall from henceforth be as followeth (vizt.)
Two venison pasties, not exceeding 30s.
A dozen of Fowles roasted
3 large apple pyes
Fruit
Two dozen of wine

There must have been some trouble when the guests assembled, for in preparation for the Lord Mayor's Day dinner next month, the following order was made:

5 Oct. 1704 Noe assistant shall bring any person to dine at the Hall on Lord Mayor's day except his wife and one servant, on penalty of ten shillings. And noe Liveryman shall bring any person save his wife on like penalty of ten shillings.

And noe master shall give unto his own or any other servant any meat from off the Table on the like penalty of ten shillings.

And the Master & Wardens & two youngest Assistants shall see all the Tables cover'd & all persons put out that are disallow'd by the above menconed orders.

It is unfortunate that we never learn what the wine was. One fears it was sometimes unsatisfactory because, on 9th October 1705, it was ordered that "the Master & Wardens doe assist in choosing wine for the dinner." On that occasion they reverted to the old standard meal, except that there were nine "messes" of everything except wild-fowl, of which only seven were supplied.

Lord Mayor's Day was always a notable one in the City Companies' year. On their return from Westminster and after watching the Lord Mayor's final progress through the City streets, the members of the Company made haste to the feast in the Hall. Attempts to restrict the numbers at the tables were not always successful. In 1709 there were several offenders who had abused an order passed "against bringing persons to Dinner that are not invited." Mr. Atkinson was heavily fined the sum of £7, Mr. Gilbert got off lightly with £1 and Mr. Smithsend was fined £2. 10s. For a time the Court seems to have changed its mind and to have excluded the wives (and servants) of members from the feast in the Hall, a step which led to protests and some sort of stay-away strike.

There were moments when a fit of parsimony gravely diminished the attractions of a Company dinner:

> *17 Oct. 1710* That 6 surloyns of beef, with Bread & Strong Beer, be provided by the Warden on Lord Mayor's Day & the dinner to be ready on the Table by 12 a clock.

Views about economising evidently swayed as the Master or the Court felt inclined, but by 1724 a reasonable line seems to have been taken:

> *13 Oct. 1724* Ordered, upon due consideration, that the bill of fare for the Lord Mayor's Day should be a sufficient number of surloyns of beef, hams, and fowles, and fruit, as to the Master & Wardens should seem meet, and that instead of the former bill of fare; – and ordered also that no apprentice or servants be admitted that day, and that no money shall be expended at Mr. Trueby's on the Company's account.

The sting in this last sentence lies in the fact that in the previous year Mr. Trueby, who used to provide for the Company on Lord Mayor's Day, put in a little bill for £66. 6s. 6d. down to 1722 and this caused a great shock to the unhappy Renter Warden of the day. The Register of Accounts shows that on 22nd August 1722, Mr. Trueby received £96. 12s. 0d. Retribution overtook him and after some years we read of a payment to "the assignees of Mr. Trueby the Vintner."

The earliest menu preserved by the Company is a short one. The year was 1679, in the days of King Charles II, and it reads:

> *30th Sep. 1679* A Coppy of the Bill of Fare delivered to the Stewards.
> Pulletts, oysters, Sawcages and bacon.
> Surloynes of Beefe, Minced pyes, 3 in a dish.
> Geese, 2 in a dish, Tongues and udders.
> Capons, 3 in a dish, Tarts.

In the middle 18th-century the Court apparently lost interest in the details of menus for the dinners they were ordering, and were concerned only with the price per head, as this direction shows:

> *19 Aug. 1756* That this Court do on the next Election day dine at the Queen's head tavern in Great Queen Street at 3s 6d per head, besides wine.

Trouble with uninvited guests and disorder around the tables appears to have continued and led at last to the following drastic decision:

> *12 Dec. 1771* (Ordered to) discontinue dining at the Hall on Lord Mayor's Day comonly attended with great expence from the admission of a number of strangers, apprentices, and others, who occasion great uproar and confusion in the Hall and prevent the proper Members of the Company dining with decency, and which, in the said comittee's opinion, reflects a discredit to the Company. That therefore instead of dining at the Hall the comittee submit that it would be more eligible, when the Company return from their stand, to have a dinner provided at some Tavern at the discretion of the Master & Wardens for the time being, & that the Court of Assistants and Livery of the Compy. only be admitted to the same, with such regulations as shall be thought advisable.

What a difference there was a century later, when the Hall saw the Company at *déjeuner* on the occasion of the Duke of Edinburgh being presented with the freedom and livery of the Company on 7th February 1873. Instead of "great uproar and confusion" preventing the members "dining with decency" the scene was all quiet dignity and orderly procedure, enlivened at intervals when the military band played with due discretion. Above all, what a transformation there was from the rough and generous fare of the 18th-century to the delicate, .yet equally abundant, menu that was served that day:

153

Potage de Tortue à l'Anglaise
Potage de Tortue Clair
Saumon au Beurre de Montpellier
Mayonnaise de Homard
Faisons à l'Albion
Galantine de Dindon à la Royale
Poulets Rotis a l'Estragon   Langue de Boeuf en Aspic
Chaux froid de Perdreaux à la Bohémienne
Poulets à la Périgord
Croustade de Muviettes à la Macédoine
Aspic de Pâté de Foies Gras
Ris de Veau en Caisses à l'Albion
Pâté de Gibier à l'Essence
Célestine de Pêches à la Creme
Gelée à la Mosaique   Gelée au Rhum
Crèmes au Marasquin
Patissérie à la Francaise   Compôte d'Ananas
Bombes glacée à la Parisienne

Once again it is tantalising not to be told anything about the wines, which were briefly described as being "of every sort and of the choicest vintages." This splendid meal was supplied from the Albion Tavern, Aldersgate Street and cost the Company exactly £63. 15s. 7d.

The entertainment when the Company was invited to dine out was just as agreeable. In 1897, for example, a member of the Court, Albert Chancellor, was simultaneously the Mayor of Richmond and in that capacity he gave a banquet "to meet the Master (the Honourable Sir James Gainsford Bruce), Wardens and Court of Assistants of the Worshipful Company of Coachmakers and Coach Harness Makers." Here we are concerned with only two inches of the three full columns devoted to the evening in the *Richmond Herald*. The "high class menu" at the Star and Garter Hotel was:

Tortue clair
Tortue lié
Truite Saumonée Sauce Genévoise
Whitebait
Terrine de Cailles à la Souvaroff

Mousse de Veau à l'Italienne
Selle d'Agneau
Haricots Verts   *Pommes Noisettes*
Ponche Marguerite
Caneton Roti
Petits Poids   *Salade*
Asperges Sauce   *Mousseline*
Timbalde de Fraise à la Chantilly
Gelée Suédoise   *Petits Fours*
Bombe Metternich
Croûte au Jambon
Dessert et Cafe

In 1937, the Company's annual Livery dinner was held at the Mansion House by invitation of the Lord Mayor and, since it was the Coronation year of King George VI, ladies were present for the first time for many years. After the Second World War, the Company held Court and Livery dinners at intervals throughout the year, using the Halls of other Companies – the Tallow Chandlers', the Painter-Stainers', the Barber-Surgeons', the Pewterers', the Mercers', the Vintners', the Goldsmiths', the Armourers and the Law Society – their own hall having been destroyed.

The Livery dinner at the Mansion House continued to be the climax of the year's events. Ladies were present and the Livery wore evening dress with decorations. The presence of ladies at some of the other Livery dinners was resumed by the third Lord Kenilworth when he became Master in 1969.

As an example of the manner in which the Company dined as it approached its 300th anniversary, here is the menu for the Livery dinner held at the Mansion House on 2nd July 1974. The Master was Paul Jennens, the Lord Mayor was Sir Hugh Wontner and the principle guest was the Rt. Hon. John Peyton, Minister of Transport:

White Peaches and Shrimps in Cognac Sauce
    Château de Viré 1971
Noisettes of Lamb Princess, Gardeners' Pride
    Santenay Les Gavières 1967

155

Raspberries and Cream
   Chàteau Climens 1969
Camembert Pancakes
   Taylor, late bottled Vintage
Coffee   Turkish Delight

At Livery dinners the ceremony of the Loving Cup is observed when the Master and Wardens take wine with the members and their guests. The cup is filled with spiced wine, immemorially termed "Sack". Immediately after dinner the cup is passed round the table and each person, after he has drunk, applies a napkin to the mouth of the cup before he passes it to his neighbour. The practice is for the person with the Loving Cup to stand up and bow to his neighbour who, also standing, removes the cover with his right hand and holds it while the other drinks, a custom said to have originated in the precaution to keep the right or "dagger hand" employed so that the person who drinks may be assured of no treachery, like that practised by Elfrida on the unsuspecting King Edward the Martyr at Corfe Castle, who was slain while drinking. On passing the Loving Cup, the person who has drunk from it immediately turns his back on his neighbour until he in turn has passed the cup on, ostensibly to protect him from attack from behind while he is in the act of drinking.

14 The Company's Plate*

THE Company's collection of plate, although not so extensive as that of many other guilds, is, as regards quality of workmanship, distinctly above average. Generally speaking, the pieces are important examples of the epoch to which they belong.

One of the best of these is the Cheslyn Flagon, a large piece which both in design and ornament is unique. Above a knight's helmet on the lid is a Phoebus seated in his chariot. On the body of the flagon are shown conspicuously the arms of the Company in high relief, with the Company's crest above. The handle and the finish to the hinge are beautifully designed, whilst the modelling of the conventional plumes and the coat of arms is in the best style. It has a wide-spreading base, with large ribbed leaves. The flagon dates from about the middle of the 17th-century and was presented to the Company by Richard Cheslyn, Junior, who was appointed Clerk in 1685.†

In 1703 Samuel Wright, a currier, presented the Company with an elaborately ornamented tankard. It is an excellent specimen of the silversmith's art, the lid being raised and fluted, while the body, which is also fluted, is ornamented with conventional foliage. The name of the donor and the date of the gift are inscribed upon a panel. The hinge and handle are particularly ornate and the base has very deep moulding.‡

A porringer, presented to the Company by Edward Hutton in 1713, is in one respect – the character of its ornaments – a rarity. Like many of the works of art of the period to which it belongs (1688), it is ornamented with Chinese or Japanese figures, etc., designed in all probability in England. At that time Anglo–Chinese art was much favoured, not only in England but also on the Continent, on account of the *objects d'art* brought back by the British and Dutch East India Companies, though it was not always so successful in its execution as that which appears upon the Hutton cup.

The cup given by Edward Salisbury is both beautiful and curious. The shape is distinctly uncommon, though one or two of

* *See* Introduction.

† *See* Plate 34.

‡ *See* Plate 35.

the guilds have pieces of somewhat similar pattern. It almost has the appearance of an old porringer with the two handles removed. It is placed upon a tall base and produces a good effect. The date of this piece is somewhat doubtful, but the design and ornament are characteristic of the period from 1650 to 1680. Edward

PLATE 34
Gilt flagons: (left) date mark 1680, given by Richard Cheslyn, Junior; (right) date mark 1693, given that year by John Jacob.

158

Salisbury, a member of the Court of Assistants, is named in the second Charter (granted by James II) and the date of his election was 1687. Another Edward Salisbury was chosen Assistant in 1694. The cup is always much admired and the workmanship is very fine.

The tall cup and cover given by Samuel Aubery is dated 1677. It is referred to in the records as "A large silver drinking bowle, gilt, in a leather case; the gift of Samuel Aubery★, Esq." The donor was admitted a member of the Company in 1677, the first year of its existance. The cup is much the same in design as many

PLATE 35
Covered tankards. Left, date mark 1702, maker William Andrewes, given by Samuel Wright, courier, in 1703. Right, date marked 1712, given by Samuel Browne, coach and coach harness maker, who was Master in 1707.

★*See* Plate 2.

PLATE 36
Replica of a loving cup made by Paul de Lamerie in 1793, given in memory of Charles Mallord William Turner (Master, 1905) by his widow and son, Charles Wilfrid Mallord Turner (Master, 1946).

other cups in the possession of the City guilds, having that plain, heavy appearance and want of ornament which characterises so many of them. It was probably made by a silversmith follower of the Protector.

A large cup and cover, given by John Tovey, who was chosen Clerk in 1718, is a characteristic example of early Georgian work. These are occasionally found in the late years of Queen Anne's reign, but in the period which elapsed between the accession of George I and 1780, when George III was King, more of these plain two-handled cups were made than at any other period. It is possible that art could not in those days fashion anything else, or that the influence of the King who loved not "poets and painters" extended a chill over the silversmith's art.

Among the other treasures are a fine silver cup given by A. Kilgower and a small silver tankard, the gift of William J. Fowler, Junior. This latter piece dates from 1677 (which makes it as old as the Company) and is an excellent specimen.*

An extract from the Court minutes of 2nd September, 1706:

> Paid the churchwardn, after he had made a seizure of a piece of plate, a quarter's rate to the poor, due at Midr. last, £2. os. 8d.

It would appear from this that money was not plentiful with the guild at that time, while the minute lends colour to the suggestion that pieces of plate were often taken in this manner. If this is so, it may account for the frequent disappearances of plate which are the cause of so much regret to the Company today.

In later years the members of the Company who had "passed the Chair" did not neglect their duty, nor did they cease to evince a generous devotion to the guild. Some of them, notably George Edwards, Lt.-Col. Stowe and James Eberle, gave sums of money, which in days of distress proved invaluable and have formed the basis of the Company's investments.

Other past-Masters have given plate and some of the additions are of a very high order. Outstanding gifts to the Company have been the Master's chain and badge, presented by the Rev. H. G. Rosedale, and the Master's, Warden's and Clerk's badges given by past-Master Sir Edward Manville.

*See Plate 3.

Among the historical pieces, mention is due of the Beadle's mace, which dates from the time of King Charles II and, no doubt, was carried by the first Beadle to be appointed to the office. It is a particularly interesting example among the many which survive as treasured possessions of the various City Companies.*

There are two models of vehicles in the Coachmakers' collection. The 4ft model of the Gold State Coach is a work of art in itself because it has the elaborate carvings of figures and scrolls by Wilton and the paintings on the panels by the Florentine aritst, Giovanni Batista Cipriani, which were reproduced on the complete vehicle. Built to be the handsomest coach in the world, it was ordered for the wedding of George III and Queen Charlotte in 1762. Various designs were called for and these were used by

PLATE 37
A Company treasure. The 4' model of the Gold State Coach designed by Sir William Chambers for the wedding of George III and Queen Charlotte in 1762. The coach itself has been used for every Coronation since George IV and is kept at the Royal Mews, Buckingham Palace.

★*See* Plate 4.

William (later Sir William) Chambers, Surveyor of H.M. Board of Works, in producing the model of the final design. It is not certain who actually made the coach. Some say it was Samuel Butler of Great Queen Street, who was Master of the Coachmakers in 1768; another account claims that Queen Charlotte visited John Hatchett, who was Master in 1785, at his premises at 121 Long Acre to view the coach when it was completed. What is certain is that the model was given by Wilton's son to Robert Vezey of Bath in 1817, and it was from his grandson that the Company purchased it by subscription in 1909. This model of the "very superb" coach (as it is described in the original records) has been lent for exhibition many times and was on view at the Mansion House for a considerable time during the festivities of King George VI's Coronation. The coach itself is kept at the Royal Mews, Buckingham Palace, and has been used for every Coronation since George IV.

At the other extreme is a model of the brougham made for the Lord Chancellor himself in 1838. This is only eight-and-a-half inches long, but the workmanship is so fine that the proportions are as perfect as in the case of the more stately coach.

A valued possession is an ivory gavel, silver mounted, which has interesting associations with transport of days past. It was the gift of Mr. J. C. Mitchell, past-Master. Fashioned as the hub of an omnibus wheel, it has one spoke attached which makes the handle. Formerly it was the property of the Camden Town Omnibus Association and after them of the Associated Omnibus Company and was used at their meetings.

15 Links with the Services

THROUGHOUT its history, the Coachmakers' Company has made up in originality and initiative for what it has lacked in rich endowments. Although its charitable bequests are negligible compared with those of "The Great Twelve", its activities in other directions have never been lacking in goodwill and warmth of fellowship.

Nothing has demonstrated this better than the "adoption" of Service units in recent years, starting in 1955 with H.M.S. *Centaur*, a light fleet carrier of 26,000 tons. (In 1947 a tentative contact had been made with the Services when the Company presented a shield bearing its Coat of Arms to H.M.S. *Anson*).

To commemorate the adoption of *Centaur*, the Company presented a mace, sash and gauntlets for use by the Drum Maj. of the ship's volunteer band, followed by the gift of a bugle. Members of the Company paid their first visit to *Centaur* at Portsmouth when she was in dry dock. Luncheon was taken with Capt. H. C. N. Rolfe, R.N., in his cabin.

A later visit coincided with a sea trial, during which the Coachmakers enjoyed a full programme of operations carried out by aircraft, helicopters, rescue and supply ships. On returning, the port authority signalled that passengers must be landed by tender. However, Capt. Horace Law, R.N., (who had succeeded Capt. Rolfe in 1958) was not known as "Hard Over" Law for nothing. He signalled "No. These City gentlemen are not to be treated like that." Despite poor visibility and the vast overhang of the ship, Capt. Law brought *Centaur* alongside the quay with superb judgement. In time he became Admiral Sir Horace Law, Cmdr.-in-Chief, Naval Home Command in 1970–72 and was elected a liveryman of the Company in 1962.

Unfortunately *Centaur* was withdrawn from service in 1970, though remaining one of Her Majesty's ships. The Company therefore asked the Board of Admiralty in 1974 if they could transfer their gifts to another ship. As a result of this request, the Company adopted H.M.S. *Hermes*, a commando ship which was originally a sister ship of *Centaur*. She was laid down at Barrow-in-Furness in 1944 and was launched in 1953 by Lady Churchill, commissioning as a fixed-wing aircraft carrier in 1959. She was converted to her present role between 1970 and 1973 and was re-commissioned by Lady Soames in 1973. The Royal Navy describes her role as follows:

> *Hermes* is officially designated as a Landing Platform, Helicopter (LPH) but is more commonly known as a Commando Ship. When operating primarily in the LPH role, with Wessex V helicopters embarked, *Hermes* can take on board, at very short notice, a full Commando group, which includes a Royal Marines Commando Detachment. This force can be landed and in action as a comprehensive unit within 2 hours, before the ship has even appeared over the horizon and the force can then be supported for a considerable time.
>
> On occasions *Hermes* may operate entirely as an anti-submarine ship, in which case only Sea King helicopters are embarked. In this capacity she makes a substantial contribution to the defence of the Fleet against underwater threat. Like her sister ship, *Bulwark*, and the Royal Navy's Assault Ships which carry heavy transport and military equipment, *Hermes* lends NATO's peace-keeping forces the capacity to intervene swiftly and effectively in a wide range of situations.*

For its next "foster child" the Company went to the Royal Air Force. In 1961 they adopted No. 216 Squadron of No. 46 Group, Strike Command. The squadron was commanded at the time by Wing-Cmdr. Norman Hoad, A.F.C., who in due course was elected to the livery. A silver rose bowl was presented to mark the adoption of the squadron and, in 1962, a silver trophy in the form of the squadron's crest. This trophy was awarded annually to the Master Aircrew and Senior Non-Commissioned Officer Aircrew Section achieving the highest aggregate Categorisation Results.

The squadron came into being as No. 16 Squadron, Royal Naval Air Service, at Manston, Kent on 8th January 1918, making the first air raid on Cologne on 24th March in the same year.

*The *Hermes* is due to have the first fully operational squadron of Sea Harriers (the Royal Navy version of the "jump jet") in 1980.

When the Royal Naval Air Service merged with the Royal Flying Corps on 1st April 1918, No. 16 Squadron R.N.A.S., became No. 216 Squardon, Royal Air Force – which is the reason why it was always referred to as "Two-Sixteen" rather than "Two-One-Six".

In July 1918 the squadron flew more than 10,000 miles in 34 raids, dropping 33 tons of bombs on the enemy. During the Second World War, the squadron evacuated the Channel Islands in the summer of 1940, dropped supplies to the defenders of Calais and moved supplies, troops and fighter wings in the North African campaign and in Burma.

After 38 years of service overseas 216 Squadron returned to England in November 1955, to be based at Lyneham in Wiltshire. Here the squadron was re-equipped with the Comet C Mark 2 aircraft, a 44 passenger jet transport, thereby becoming the first military jet transport squadron.

Much of its work was on special VIP flights, and passengers carried by "Two-Sixteen" included H.M. the Queen, Prince Philip, the Queen Mother, Princess Margaret, Harold Macmillan and President Eisenhower. In May 1952 the squadron received its Standard.

On 16th November 1974 a party of Coachmakers visited the squadron at Lyneham, flying from Gatwick by way of a quick circuit of Britain in order to give time for lunch on board. The party emerged, shaken but unscathed, from sessions in the Comet simulator (where crash landings were all too easy); and from an unscheduled visit to Swindon public baths at 7 a.m. after a guest night in the Mess – the object being to participate in the squadron's monthly exercise of climbing into an inflatable dinghy after ditching. Mercifully for the older members, swimming trunks were in short supply.

Norman Hoad's successor, Wing-Cmdr. Philip Walker, became a liveryman of the Company in 1973. It was a matter of great sadness for the Company when No. 216 Squadron became a victim of the 1975 defence cuts, and was subsequently disbanded.

Fortunately a splendid replacement for the lamented "Two-Sixteen" was found in No. 10 Squadron, R.A.F., stationed at Brize Norton, Oxfordshire. One of the Royal Flying Corps' original squadrons, No. 10 was formed at Farnborough on 1st January 1915.

After moving to Brooklands and then to Hounslow, the squadron was re-equipped with BE2Cs at Netheravon and sent to France for reconnaisance work in support of the British First Army.

The squadron was in action throughout the First World War, seeing service at the battles of Loos, the Somme, Arras and Ypres and bombing (with six 40 lb. bombs) by day and, later, by night. In 1917 they were re-equipped with Armstrong Whitworths.

After the First World War the squadron was disbanded, and it has been revived and disbanded several times since. It became part of the bomber force at Upper Heyford, Oxfordshire, with Handley Page Hyderabads in 1928 (a year before "HP" joined the Livery) and was one of the first squadrons to receive the Handley Page Heyford bomber. In 1937 it was moved north from Boscombe Down to Dishforth, Yorkshire where it was given Armstrong Whitworth Whitleys.

In 1939, five days after war was declared, the squadron made its first sortie over Germany – a leaflet raid. For the rest of the war No. 10 was on active bombing duty over Norway, Germany, France, the Low Countries and Italy (it was the first R.A.F. squadron to cross the Alps).

In 1941 the Whitleys were replaced with Halifaxes. These aircraft took part in the first 1,000 bomber raid on Cologne and in the massive raids on Essen, Hamburg and Berlin. Two years later the squadron shared in the raids on the flying bomb and rocket establishment at Peenemunde on the German Baltic coast north of Berlin. The squadron operated from Yorkshire throughout the war and was commanded for a time by Wing-Cmdr. Don Bennett (later, Air Vice-Mshl. Bennett). He was later to command the Pathfinder Force, in which the Tercentenary Master of the Coachmakers, Wing-Cmdr. Maurice Smith, D.F.C., and bar, was a distinguished member.

After the Second World War the disbandments and revivals were resumed, beginning with disbandment in 1947 at the end of a period of service in India and Pakistan, flying Dakota transport aircraft. The squadron was reformed in 1953 for four years, during which it flew Canberra bombers and, after a year's disbandment, it was revived again in 1958 as a Victor V-bomber squadron. Disbanded once more in 1964, just after being presented with its Standard by H.R.H. Princess Margaret, No. 10

was reformed in 1966 for its present role flying VC-10s in which it has carried Her Majesty the Queen, members of the Royal Family and many VIPs.

Much of the squadron's activity is devoted to maintaining a high state of mobility, in order to provide a global strategic air-lift for all three Services. The squadron demonstrated its cap-ability in another sphere when it was involved in the massive withdrawal of families and refugees from Cyprus during the Turkish invasion in 1974.

The question of adopting an Army unit had been raised in 1962, but had presented certain difficulties in the selection of a suitable formation.

It was left to Paul Jennens, when he was Master in 1974, to find the happy solution of adopting the 4th/7th Royal Dragoon Guards, in which Maj. Michael Dangerfield, a member of the Livery and son of a past-Master, was a serving officer. To com-memorate the adoption, the Company presented the regiment with a new Standard on the occasion of the 50th Annual Cavalry Memorial Parade held in Hyde Park on Sunday, 5th May 1974. The 4th/7th formed part of the parade of 3,400 men, representing 14 cavalry regiments of the line, who were reviewed by H.R.H. the Prince of Wales. At a subsequent Court dinner, Maj.-Gen. Ian Gill, the Colonel of the 4th/7th, who had personally received the Standard from the Master, told the members that the Company's Standard "shone out above all others" at the Band-stand where the service was held and was the envy of all other regiments. Gen. Gill and Lt.-Col. Robert Baddeley, the Commanding Officer, were elected liverymen of the Company in 1974.

The 4th/7th Royal Dragoon Guards were formed in 1922 when the 4th Royal Irish Dragoon Guards and the 7th (Princess Royal's) Dragoon Guards were combined into one regiment. The 4th, originally called the Earl of Arran's Horse, was formed by James II in 1685, eight years after the Company received its first Charter. After making a name for itself fighting against the French in Holland, the regiment moved to Ireland in 1798 where it stayed for the next 100 years, being called the 1st Irish Horse before taking its final name. (They were also known as the "Blue Horse" from the colour of their coat facings and the "Mounted Micks" because so many of them were Irish.)

In 1789 the regiment was sent to Spain, earning its first battle honour, Peninsula, in Wellington's Army and losing 239 men and 445 horses before returning home in 1811. In 1854 the regiment was in the Crimea serving as part of the Heavy Brigade, which charged 3,500 Russian cavalry with only 500 men. When it seemed all was lost, Gen. Scarlet released the 4th Dragoon Guards, who had been held in reserve until then. They charged, crashing into the flank of the Russians who broke and fled.

Active service in Egypt, India and South Africa followed, and when the First World War broke out on 4th August 1914 the regiment was in France within 12 days as part of the British Expeditionary Force. Six days later a patrol of the 4th took part in the first action between British and German troops near Mons. The patrol leader, Capt. Hornby, was the first man to draw blood with the sword and Corp. Thorn fired the first shot of the war.

The regiment took part in the battles at Ypres (where it lost nearly half its strength in one operation), Arras and Cambrai, and when the Armistice was signed in November 1918 it was within 10 miles of where it had started in August 1914. In the final German offensive in 1918, which the Allies held, the regiment lost 175 officers and men killed.

The Princess Royal's Dragoon Guards originated as Devonshire's Horse (ranking as the 10th Horse) in 1689, the Duke of Devonshire having been commissioned to form a regiment of horse as a reward for helping William III in his invasion of England. In Ireland a few years later they fought at the Battle of the Boyne as Schonberg's Horse (having changed their Colonel), afterwards fighting in Europe under King William.

After a short time in England, the regiment returned to the Continent as part of the Duke of Marlborough's Army, being present at all his great victories: Blenheim, Ramilles, Oudenarde and Malplaquet. Back in Ireland the regiment came under the command of Col. Ligioner, who later became a Field Marshal and Commander-in-Chief of the British Army.

In 1742 Ligioner's Horse were in Europe once more, fighting with distinction against the French at Dettingen where the Standard Bearer, Cornet Richardson, suffered 37 sabre cuts and bullet wounds. In 1789, after three years in the Seven Years War during which they were rather confusingly called the 4th Irish Horse (the "Black Horse" on account of their black tunic facings), the regiment was given its final name, the 7th (Princess Royal's) Dragoon Guards. During Victoria's reign, the regiment saw service in the 7th Kaffir War and the Arabi Pasha campaign before going to South Africa for the Boer War. They were present at Diamond Hill and helped to capture the Boer Government along with nearly £12,000 in cash.

The start of the First World War found the regiment in Egypt. It was sent direct to France, landing at Marseilles in tropical uniform in November. Although spending most of the time in trench warfare, the 7th managed to retain their mounted role for occasional actions (at Cambrai in 1917, for example), and making a full cavalry advance in the August, 1918, offensive during which they captured many prisoners and guns. They captured a bridge at Lessines in Belgium only 10 minutes before the Armistice was signed.

For the combined 4th/7th the inter-war years were spent as a horsed cavalry regiment, at first in India and then at home. The last mounted parade took place near Edinburgh in 1938, though a mounted squadron was sent to Palestine on internal security duties for a short time afterwards.

By 1939 the first light tanks and Bren gun carriers had arrived and mechanised training was in full swing. The 4th/7th shared in the general misery of the retreat from France in 1940, suffering heavy casualties to men and vehicles. Reformed in England with Covenanter tanks, the regiment later switched to Shermans and returned to France, landing on D-Day in June 1944. By the end of the day they were six miles inland.

The August advance found them "swanning" across France and into Belgium, then on to Holland and the Rhine. There followed the long, frustrating winter before the final advance was made into Germany during the spring of 1945. The 4th/7th had their final victory parade in Bremerhaven under the eyes of the Commander of 30 Corps, Gen. Brian Horrocks.

Since the end of the Second World War the 4th/7th Royal Dragoon Guards have served in Palestine, the Middle East, North Germany, Aden, Northern Ireland and Cyprus, returning to Germany in 1969 for four years where they were equipped with Chieftain tanks.

The Coachmakers' Company paid their first visit to the 4th/7th at Tidworth on 12th September 1975. One of the party recorded his impression:

One wonders, rather guiltily sometimes, whether we or our adopted service units get the greater enjoyment from our association, for it would be hard to imagine a pleasanter day than ours with the 4th/7th Royal Dragoon Guards. Our particular pleasure is at least in part owed to the extraordinary *rapport* that exists between officers and men; and the comradeship, loyalty and even dedication that one sees – in an England where an atmosphere of strikes, discontent and, worse still, violence is more the norm.

The 20 Coachmakers who went to Tidworth – apart from the lavish hospitality they received – saw an impressive drive past of Chieftain tanks, Ferret scout cars and guided weapons carriers, following an inspection by the Colonel of the Regiment, Maj-Gen. Ian Gill. After drinks in the Corporals' Mess and lunch in the Officers' Mess, some of us were trustingly let loose at the controls of the Chieftain tanks. Most of us, lowering ourselves through the small hatch into the driving seat, had acute misgivings that we might break something. "Not a chance", we were told, "they are soldier proof!"

The highlight of the day, so far as the Coachmakers were concerned, was the final round in the Coachmakers' Prize competition, presented to promote initiative and determination of Troop Leaders in their responsibilities towards training their own men. All troops in the regiment take part and the subjects include fitness, first-aid, signals, nuclear/chemical warfare, small-arms shooting, vehicle recognition and map reading. The final round was a formidable assault course, through and over which the participants hurled themselves with extraordinary agility and courage – and appropriate shouts of encouragement. Prizes were presented to Troop Leaders by the Master – £50 for first place, £30 for second and £20 for third. The Master also presented the Heslop Cup, traditionally awarded for inter-Troop competitions.

During their visit to the 4th/7th, a Corporal approached one of the Coachmakers' party. "Could you possibly", he asked, "use your influence in motor sport to get us a car and, maybe, some sponsorship, for entering international rallies?" Knowing

171

the extremely high driving standards required, and the scarcity of sponsors nowadays, the liveryman promised to do something – but offered little hope of success. Back at his office he telephoned Stuart Turner, the Ford Motor Company's Director of Motor Sport, who immediately offered to take the Corporal as a non-paying pupil at the newly opened Ford training centre for rally drivers, a course that normally costs £30. This generous offer was taken up by the 4th/7th, who wrote an official and charming letter of gratitude to the Coachmakers.

Except for the few private drags driven by members of the Coaching Club, which had been founded in 1871, horse-drawn vehicles gradually disappeared from the roads when motor cars started to be made in large numbers after the First World War. There was no fun in driving a gig or dog cart in fast-moving traffic, but these vehicles came in useful during the Second World War when there was no petrol for private motoring.

As a result of the interest in horse-drawn vehicles following H.M. The Queen's Coronation in 1953, some people's thoughts were turned back to the leisurely enjoyment of driving in the countryside. After a historical pageant of carriages at the Royal Agricultural Society's Show, when it was held in Windsor Great Park in 1954, Col. Arthur Main, Capt. Frank Gilbey and Sanders Watney decided in 1956 to form the British Driving Society as a focal point for this renewed interest.

Sanders Watney was elected President and has held this office ever since. The inaugural meet was held at the Royal Windsor Horse Show in 1959, when some 30 vehicles paraded round the ring before setting off on a five-mile drive through the Home Park.

The demand for the Society's help and encouragement far exceeded the modest hopes of the organisers. Instead of the few hundred members they had expected, they found themselves with a 1,000 within ten years. The 1,000th member was Princess Anne, who "drove herself in" with a pair of Haflingers to a pony chaise at a meet at Smith's Lawn, Windsor Great Park, in 1969 – the first time the Society had been invited to use this beautiful ground. Today the Society's membership stands at about 2,000. Prince Philip is the Patron and Prince Charles has recently joined.

There are all kinds of events for the driving enthusiast. Meets are held in many parts of the country both by the B.D.S. and by regional driving clubs. These are non-competitive and consist of a long-distance drive with perhaps a stop for tea or a picnic lunch.

173

Wherever possible they are held on roads closed to ordinary traffic for it is along private gravel lanes and forestry enclosures that the serene pleasure of driving as it used to be before the arrival of the motor car can be recaptured.

Like all country sports, driving is classless and is based on a shared enthusiasm for an activity which is in harmony with Nature. The driving club picnics and suppers after the meets provide a social life of their own.

Then there are the show classes for vehicles at many agricultural and county shows, again organised with the aid of the Society. After a parade in the main ring with an inspection of turnout, the competitors leave for a short driving Marathon of between five and ten miles. On their return to the ring the vehicles are finally judged. At some shows there are similar classes for four-in-hand coaches which add to the picturesqueness of the scene.

Driving at its most expert is seen in the events held under the rules of the Fédération Equestre Internationale. These begin with the judging of presentation (turn-out), followed by dressage in harness. On the next day there is a cross-country Marathon of anything up to 25 miles, including formidable hazards, and the event – which lasts three days – ends with a timed obstacle course.

As President of the F.E.I. Prince Philip was responsible for the introduction of these driving competitions into England, and has himself taken part with considerable success in many of them. His active interest in driving began in 1971 soon after he was guest of honour at a dinner held in the Great Hall at Hampton Court to celebrate the centenary of the Coaching Club. Sanders Watney was the president on that occasion (and later had the honour of being accompanied on the box seat by H.R.H.) but he retired in 1975 and was succeeded by Lieutenant-Colonel Sir John Miller, the Crown Equerry.

In 1971 the European three-day driving championships under F.E.I. rules were held in Windsor Great Park in conjunction with the Royal Windsor Horse Show. The Coachmakers' Company joined with the Saddlers' in donating a set of harness as a prize. In the following year the World driving championships were held at Munster in West Germany, where Great Britain won the team gold medal. Two years later, in 1974, this success was repeated when these championships were held in Switzerland.

Not to be mentioned in the same breath is the new sport called "scurry driving". This timed obstacle test is much to the liking of television sports programme producers, who doubtless see in it a pale shadow of Roman chariot racing. But some traditionalists deprecate the fact that the beautiful old vehicles which were not made for high speeds over rough ground are liable to be irreparably damaged in this sport, although this has been largely avoided by the introduction of purpose-built modern carriages. Nevertheless, the scramble round an indoor flood-lit arena is as far removed from the traditionally elegant method of driving along the country road as can be imagined.

It would be interesting to know who made the veteran vehicles that turn out in such numbers at driving events. Many must be the work of members of the Coachmakers' Company in the last century – Mr. and Mrs. Sanders Watney, for example, have a gig

PLATE 38
Drawing of a four-in-hand coach (private drag) made by Cockshoot in 1897 and now owned by Frank Gillam, a member of the Company.

175

made by Lawton-Goodman; while a member of the Livery, Jack Gillam, an ex-chairman of the British Driving Society, has a magnificent park drag which was made in 1897 by Cockshoots of Manchester for a Mr. Waud of Bradford for use on his honeymoon. This massive vehicle, which cost 350 guineas and took four months to build, has a luncheon box on the roof and an imperial (a kind of luggage trunk) containing a water tank which supplies both a wash basin as well as a commode under the seat inside the vehicle.

The growing popularity of driving has outrun the availability of old vehicles. Although they are still unearthed in remote country houses and farms from time to time and lovingly restored by specialist firms, the supply does not meet the demand. In fact the national "stock" of old vehicles is being continuously depleted by enthusiasts who come from all over the world to bid high prices for the vehicles that come on the market at auction sales. The firm of Thimbleby and Shorland, for example, hold regular sales at Reading and at their last auction in 1976 there were visitors from Australia, the United States and the Continent to bid for the 140 horse-drawn vehicles and 117 sets of harness on offer. Two park drags in splendid condition went to a French buyer – one by Henry Whitlock for £4,400 and another by Fred Allen for £5,000 – while an American visitor paid £1,800 for a Burton-style van by Jones of Hereford. Most of the English private driving harness was snapped up by buyers from abroad.

Now the wheel has turned full circle, and a few small firms are making replicas of gigs, phaetons, dog carts and other vehicles to order. The craft of coachmaking has come to life again. The painstaking methods employed by one of these firms are described by Peter Garnier in the next chapter.

17 The Old and the New*

SOMEWHERE, in most of us, there exists a love for old things and old ways. Among the latest manifestations of this feeling is the revival of driving. Since the supply of old vehicles in good conditions is necessarily limited, there is a steadily increasing demand for vehicles built to the old styles, but using modern materials, techniques and equipment.

To meet this demand a new coachmaking trade has sprung up, consisting of a score of small firms and individuals variously engaged in restoring old vehicles, making "one-offs" to special order, and in a few cases turning them out in quite considerable numbers. The Harewood Carriage Company, for example, has produced more than 250 private driving carriages since it was started six years ago by Stanley Johnson in North Devon, tucked away in the Holsworthy Industrial Estate. They are fully booked with orders for nine months ahead, though they have not advertised for a couple of years. Three-quarters of their production goes overseas and they estimate that the world market for such vehicles amounts to £750,000 a year.

It is not Johnson's policy to carry out restorations or build replicas in the puristic sense; the work by Harewood is all new construction of old designs. They could, for example, very easily use square-headed, mild steel "blacksmith's" bolts, but to do so would be to simulate antiquity and, in Johnson's view, would be dishonest. Instead, they use high-tensile hexagon-headed nuts and bolts, on the principle that the old carriage makers would have used them if they'd had them. Modern marine-plywood is used for the panels and major structures – which is not as out-of-keeping as it may seem, since laminated plywood was first developed for the carriage trade. All the metal-work is made at Holsworthy, including the complicated fore-carriage with its full elliptic springing and steering gear ("fifth wheel" to the articulated commercial vehicle user), and the complete under-frame at the back – all the running gear, in fact; only the springs themselves are bought out. All these metal parts are based on

*See Introduction.

177

original designs, a priceless reference book being William Adams's *Illustrated List of Coach Ironwork*, dated 1870; Adams, who supplied the coachbuilding trade, had premises in Lord Street, Birmingham.

Perhaps the most surprising thing about Harewood is the variety of vehicles built or currently building. One overseas order is for a fully covered, carved and gilded State ceremonial coach, along the lines of the Coronation Coach. This large, coachman-driven vehicle is an exception, the normal demand being for the light types of open, owner-driven vehicles. In the two-wheeler class there are Cut-under, Spindle-back, Step-in, Liverpool and Round-back Gigs, (all two-seaters), Ralli-Car, Norfolk Car and Dog Cart (all four-seaters). The Dog Cart is also found among

PLATE 39.
Two of the principal vehicles now being produced by the Harewood Carriage Company in North Devon: (left) *the two-wheel dog-cart;* (right) *the roof-seat break.*

178

the four-wheelers, together with the Wagonette (six seats), Game Cart (four seats), Roof-seat Break (seven seats), Boot-seat Victoria (six seats), Spider Phaeton (three seats), King George IV Phaeton (four seats), Vis-à-Vis (four seats), Landau (four seats plus driver and groom), and Hansom Cab (two seats and driver). Like so many vehicles of their period, they are remarkable for their light build – thanks to the road-engineering advances by Telford and Macadam and the adoption of the elliptic spring by Obadiah Elliott, which together were largely responsible for the lightness and elegance that characterised British carriages and made their builders famous.

When a customer has decided the type of vehicle he wants – a decision arrived at by reference to several contemporary cata-logues of early carriage makers – working drawings are prepared. Since, unfortunately, there is no "British Standard Horse", the customer's particular animal becomes the datum. If someone wants a Spindle-back Gig for example (a 210 lb. sporting two-seater for young men in the 1890s – the E-Type Jaguar of its day) for a 15-hand horse, this gives the draft-line dimensions – the size of the shafts. Thereafter, basing the drawings on the cata-logue illustration, and achieving an aesthetic balance between the relative masses – the horse included – the vehicle is drawn up. When the vehicle is not intended for use in competitive events and the overall appearance is not so critical, accurate measure-ments are taken from a vehicle in a museum.

The shafts are built-up, laminated and, on the little two-seaters, amazingly flexible to damp out the trotting motion of the horse. On the big four-wheelers such as the Roof-seat Break with its team of four 16-hand horses, the two "wheelers" are harnessed by traces to the splinter-bar and the two "leaders" to the pole which, in turn, is attached to the turning member of the fore-carriage, all four horses being insulated from the vehicle by their harness. This introduces a problem with braking. In driving events the 20–25km cross-country courses include down-grades demanding brakes – usually the conventional shoe-type acting on the rear wheels – since the horses in team harness cannot hold the vehicle back. The dressage test, in turn, requires the vehicle to run up and stop dead, standing still for 30 sec. without the driver's touching the brakes. Since a high-spirited team will not readily stand still, and since there is no ban on disc brakes, there

is a tendency for some entrants to fit hydraulically operated discs – with a separate foot pedal tucked away beneath an apron. And, since it needs two hands to control the horses anyway, why not use the footbrake on the downhill sections too? What if it *will* pull the spokes out – you can always have specially built steel wheels, with oval tubular spokes? There must be problems, however, with the location of the rear axle which, with its full elliptic springing, is pretty flexible.

PLATE 40

Shafts for two-wheel vehicles. Getting the cross-section right after laminating the blanks. In the background, finishing a lead-bar to which the leader horses in a four-in-hand are harnessed, the lead-bar being attached to the pole-fitting.

The wheels themselves are one of the most interesting aspects of this present day carriage making. Basically, as in the past, the spokes are dished outwards to give lateral stiffness, so that the tyre is almost outboard of the hub. The axle ends have a $3\frac{1}{2}$-degree downward sett, the bottoms of the wheels being appreciably closer together than the tops – so that the downward pointing spoke is always roughly vertical to the ground, and the tyre is

PLATE 41
Trimming up after the final assembly of a wheel for a two-wheel dog cart. The epoxy resin hub can be seen with the tubular metal "hub bond". Originally shrunk on to the wooden hub to prevent splitting, this now serves only for effect.

always flat to it. In construction, however, the wheels are far from traditional. They were made up in 45-degree ash segments or felloes (pronounced "felleys") so that there were eight segments. Two-wheelers always had 16 spokes, of oak, or two per felloe; four-wheelers had 14 in the rear wheels and 12 in the front. The spokes were traditionally let into the felloes, the felloes themselves being butt-jointed together and held in place by a shrunk on steel band or tire (tyre). The concentricity of the wheel depended on the skill of the wheelwright; once the tyre was in place, the wheel could not be re-trued.

Harewood have patented their own method of wheel construction, the wheel becoming a structure in its own right with the tyre providing additional strength – and a protection against wear. The felloes themselves are no thicker than the ends of the spokes that fit into them, with a separate felloe between each pair of spokes. The felloes are butt-jointed together at the entry points of the spokes; then, on either side of the felloes, with their own butt-joints half-way between each pair of spokes, come additional ash laminations, the whole structure being held together with a two-part resourcinol resin glue – like Aerolite 365. It is then turned true and protected by a shrunk-on steel tyre. The ultimate result is exactly the same as the traditional method, but much stronger. On the larger four-wheelers, such as the seven-seater Roof-seat Break, with its "dry" weight of 6 cwt., the wheels are metal shod. But the ligher two- and four-wheeler sporting vehicles have rubber tyres, as they are quieter on the roads and more settling for the horse.

The hubs are made by an even more unorthodox method of construction than is used for the wheels. Instead of being turned in the traditional elm, they are cast in an epoxy resin, and fitted with ball-bearings.

Coach painting, in contrast, is traditional from start to finish, and is done by brush; there is no paint spraying equipment in the buildings. The paint is supplied as ground pigment, made up as an oil-bound "putty". Sufficient of this is dissolved in white spirit to make a "paintable" consistency; and it is strained before each new coat is applied. The bare wood, after very careful preparation, is given one coat of primer, after which any irregularities are filled with a stopper filler applied with a palette knife. When all this has dried hard it is rubbed down, using a flat block for the wet and dry rubbing down paper; any undulations would be emphasised if the fingers were used without the block, and this use of a block and wet and dry paper continues throughout the process.

Next come four or five coats of primer filler, each rubbed down with progressively finer papers until the surface is thought to be dead flat. After this comes the "guide coat" – a very diluted coat of the final colour – which is lightly rubbed down. If it comes off in patches, the surface is not level enough and further coats of primer filler are applied, each rubbed down and checked with a guide coat. When the surface has been thoroughly prepared to a dead flat, matt surface, the colour coats are applied – three or four of them, each rubbed down with progressively finer paper, until an all over flat, matt surface has been achieved in the final colour.

This is followed by a coat of flatting varnish, which is rubbed down as before, but using soap to prevent clogging. At this stage, the coach lining is applied – with unerring and unhesitating accuracy – and the whole job given a second coat of flatting varnish. This is again rubbed down before the final, critical coat of varnish is applied. The ambient temperature, and the temperature of the varnish, must be just right – at 65°F. It must not be put on too sparingly or you get brush lines; and too lavishly produces "runs", though it is principally the manner in which the oval varnish brush is "drawn off" that avoids these.

An alternative method of achieving the final finish – after the "guide coat" stage – is to apply the first colour coat, rub it down, and then apply a second coat with a 10 per cent proportion of varnish. The proportion of colour is progressively reduced through four or five stages, until the final coat of pure varnish is applied – each successive coat, of course, being rubbed down. The varnish brushes are kept suspended in linseed oil – never washed out. All the impurities fall to the bottom of the "brush keep"; and before using, the brushes are pressed free of excess linseed oil. The old coach builders used never to paint the undersides of their vehicles, nor the insides where the timber was hidden by upholstery, in order to allow the wood to breathe. The decision nowadays is left to the customer's choice.

So far as timber is concerned – ash, beech and oak – this is very difficult to obtain fully seasoned, so it is bought as standing trees and brought into the workshops as necessary for its five years' seasoning. The major part of the vehicles is built up of marine ply, without the need for extensive framing, as generally the design of the bodies provides a strong box-section – such as the transverse "luggage-locker" beneath the seats of the Dog-carts, with its louvred ends to admit air to the hunt-terriers and gun-dogs that travel traditionally inside. It is interesting that on some of the little two-wheelers, the "dashing board", which protected the occupants from mud thrown up when the horses were dashing, was eventually to form a convenient "dash-board" for the instruments on the early cars.

Tools used at Harewood are, of course, completely modern – circular and band saws, electric hand tools and sanders, routing machines, high-speed millers and anything else that is available. And arc- and gas-welding are used instead of the old blacksmiths' hammer-welding methods, complicated metal parts like the pole-head fitting being appreciably more elegant as a result. "Tyres" – of $\frac{3}{8}$ in., mild steel strip – are rolled on a three-roller machine, which "breaks the back" of the strip as it runs through, and cut to the exact circumference of the wheel. A few file cuts are then taken off the ends to reduce the finished circumference to a shrink-fit on the wheel; then the ends are welded together. Where rubber tyres are fitted, the mild steel base has a "clincher channel", or internal dovetail, into which the external dovetail of the tyre fits.

Harewood are essentially carriagemakers, as distinct from coachmakers – the difference being that a coach was driven by a coachman, and Harewood's products are owner-driven. Also, a coach was closed; but a carriage was open – or could be open or closed by virtue of its folding hood. Exceptions are the Brougham and Landau which, being closed, are coaches; but they can be either owner- or coachman-driven.

On looking through the wealth of old catalogues, books and other publications down at Holsworthy, and reading of the speed and regularity of the stage- and mail-coaches in the old days, one wondered whether – with modern roads, methods and materials – these achievements could be improved upon. Would an *Exeter Telegraph* of the 1970s beat the $17\frac{3}{8}$ hours regularly taken for the 176 miles from Piccadilly to Exeter – including meal stops and 18 changes of horses? And would the London–Devonport *Quicksilver* improve on the old 11.5 m.p.h. average speed, which included meal stops and 21 changes – at 45 sec. per change?

Having read of the lengthy and painstaking finishing methods used by carriage- and coach-builders of the past and present day, readers may be interested in the following care and maintenance instructions to coachmen, extracted from an article *Hints for the Preservation of a Carriage* that appeared in *The Hub*, published in New York in the 1870s:

> A carriage should be kept in an airy, dry coach-house, with a moderate amount of light; otherwise the colours will be destroyed.
>
> There should be no communication between the stables and the coach-house. The manure-heap or pit should also be kept as far away as possible. Ammonia cracks varnish, and fades the colours both of the painting and lining.
>
> Whenever standing for days together, a carriage should always have on it a large cotton cover, sufficiently strong to keep off the dust without excluding the light. Dust, when allowed to settle on a carriage, eats into the varnish. Care should be taken to keep this cover dry.
>
> When a carriage is new or newly-painted, it is better for it to stand a few weeks before being used. It will stain or spot, even then, unless care be taken to remove the mud before it dries on, or as soon afterwards as possible. A carriage should never, under any circumstances, be put away dirty.
>
> In washing a carriage, keep it out of the sun, and have the lever of the "setts" covered with leather. Use plenty of water, taking great care that it is not driven into the body, to the injury of the lining. Use for the body a large, soft sponge; when saturated squeeze this over the panels, and by the flowing down of the water the dirt will soften and harmlessly run off; then finish with a soft chamois leather.
>
> The same remarks apply to the under-parts and wheels. Never use a "spoke brush", which, in conjunction with the grit from the road, acts like sandpaper on the varnish. Scratching it, and of course removing the gloss. If persisted in, it will rub off the varnish and paint even down to the wood. Never allow water to dry itself

on a carriage as it invariably leaves stains.

Enamelled-leather heads and aprons should be washed with soap and water, and then rubbed very lightly with linseed oil.

In cleaning brass or silver, no acid, mercury, or grit should be used; the polish should be obtained solely by friction.

To prevent or destroy moths in woolen linings, use turpentine and camphor. In a close carriage the evaporation from this mixture, when placed in a saucer, the glasses being up, is a certain cure.

Be careful to grease the bearings of the fore-carriage so as to allow it to turn freely. If it turn with difficulty, the shafts or pole will be liable to strain or break.

Examine the carriage occasionally, and whenever a bolt or clip appears to be getting loose tighten it up with a wrench, and always have little repairs done at once. Should the tires of the wheels get at all slack, so that the joints of the felloes are seen, have them immediately contracted, or the wheels may be permanently injured. "A stitch in time saves nine!"

Examine the axles; keep them well oiled, and see that the washers are in good order. Castor oil is considered the best for oiling; sperm oil will answer; but never use sweet oil, as it will gum up. Be careful in taking off the axle-nuts not to cross the threads or strain them when replaced.

Keep a small bottle of black japan and a brush always handy, to paint the treads and steps when worn by the feet; nothing helps more than this to keep a carriage looking tidy. Lay on the japan as thin as possible.

Never draw a carriage out of, or back it into, a coach-house with the horses attached, as more accidents occur from this than any other cause.

Headed carriages should never stand with the head down; and aprons of every kind should be frequently unfolded or they will soon spoil.

As a general rule, a carriage, with gentle work, retains its freshness better than if standing for the long periods in a coach-house. If the latter be necessary, draw the carriage out occasionally to air.

See that the coach-house doors can be so fastened as not to blow to by the wind.

Do not use oil cloths in carriages. Covering the bottoms of carriages with oil cloths is a fruitful source of trouble, causing, as it does, the bottoms to rot by retaining the moisture between the wood and the cloth. Any article that is air-tight should not be used unless care is taken to remove it when the carriage is not in use. Grass mats are more cleanly and comfortable and less injurious.

18 Old Car Restoration*

IN a helter-skelter world of cheap, buy-use-and-replace motoring, there is neither time nor money, we are told, for craftsmanship. Worse still, such craftsmen are discouraged. A man can earn more bashing-out, filling and respraying accident-damaged cars than he can by learning, perfecting and using the old coachbuilding skills. But fortunately a few people have come to terms with themselves and decided that "job satisfaction" is more important to them than money. And a few others, having placed money-making high on their lists of priorities, can afford the luxury of bought-out old-car restoration. These two opposing views have found common ground in the reconstruction, or even replica-building, of wheeled antiques.

It is noteworthy that here, too, the people concerned run true to type. To the craftsman in wood or metal, the pride and satisfaction in a job well done are identical whether the chassis is a Bull-nosed Morris or a Silver Ghost Rolls-Royce. The problems and the skills are the same; even the cost to the customer is not really very different. But to the man who commissions it, the finished job represents an investment – which is why so many Rolls-Royce and Bentleys are professionally restored, and so few humbler cars. If a man has £5,000 to spend he will spend it on a Rolls-Royce because of the resale value.

Scattered round the country are a few small businesses where such craftsmanship is still encouraged. Often they are tucked away in barns and farm buildings, clear of the concrete jungles and rat-race of modern city life. As an example, we chose Keith Bowley's Ashton Keynes Vintage Restorations – not because they are superior to others, but because they are representative. We went along to the village near Cirencester on one of those golden days of the long, 1976 summer – when we should have been worrying about the drought, but weren't – and found Tony Hicks sitting in the sunshine studying the rotting remains of a Gurney Nutting coupé body that had once graced a 25 h.p. six-cylinder Rolls-Royce chassis in the mid-1930s. The badly corroded

*See Introduction.

188

aluminium panels had been removed – piecemeal. What remained
of the timber frame, with its rusted steel gussets, brackets, foot-
wells, chassis runners, shaft-tunnel and seat-pans, was being
carefully dismembered, each part being measured and recorded
in a notebook, full of beautiful little drawings. One side of the
frame work was in a far worse state than the other; it was this that
he was dismantling. If anything fell apart upon removal, which
much of it did, there was always the other side for reference.

Thus was beginning the re-creation of two replica Gurney
Nutting coachbuilt bodies, identical in almost every respect to the
original, for two Rolls-Royce 25 h.p. chassis – Tony's first experience of "quantity production". In time, the metal parts would
be shot-blasted and zinc-sprayed, to be absorbed into the timber

PLATE 42
*Used as a pattern, carefully meas-
ured and faithfully copied, this
decaying skeleton will form the
basis for two brand-new "Gurney
Nutting" coupé bodies for renovated Rolls-Royce 25 horsepower
chassis.*

frames as they grew up simultaneously on the sheet-metal chassis-runners in the workshop. With these, there would be no need to build and panel direct on to the chassis – suggesting, as was the case, that this particular body style went into limited production in its time. Body building by Gurney Nutting could therefore have gone ahead simultaneously with chassis production. With "one-off" bodies, the completed chassis and running gear had first to be delivered to the coachbuilders before their work could begin – the complete car taking a considerable time to produce.

Instead of the plain steel screws that had rusted into the timber, the fastenings on the replica bodies would be cadmium-plated; the timber itself would be treated with clear Cuprinol; in most of the old cars it seems that no preservative was used –

though they had a metal primer so tough that no paint-stripper will touch it. And such joints as could be made permanently rigid – the laminations in the A-posts, for example – would be glued with Borden, instead of the old heated Scotch glue and glue-pot. Otherwise, methods and materials would be exactly as in the original car – beech where no flexibility was needed, otherwise ash; the same joints, using screws alone where flexing was necessary; and, of course, wheel-arches would be built-up of several pieces, using overlapping butt-joints, so that the grain was always tangential.

It is not easy nowadays to obtain fully seasoned timber – a year's maturing is required for every inch of thickness – and, like everything else, the price is rising rapidly. In consequence, stocks of timber are laid in, being used progressively as they mature; 1971 stocks were being used in 1976. The only use for unseasoned, "Yonge and greene Tymber" is in hood hoops, where green ash is steamed into shape – and then left to season. Thin, curved sections in the bodywork are laminated and glued, as they were in the early days. Since this small company of specialists is concerned only with Vintage cars (31st December 1918 to 31st December 1930) the finished bodies are spray-painted in cellulose because this method was general throughout the period. Had they been concerned with the earlier Veteran or Edwardian periods, the cars would have been hand-painted, and finished – as was the practice – with warm varnish.

We moved from Tony's methodical examination of the Gurney Nutting body into the workshops where, among other cars, a replica James Young closed body on a 1925 20 h.p. Rolls-Royce was in progress, copied in every conceivable detail from another car on the premises. The timber frame had been completed – to a degree of accuracy and perfection that is hard to describe. Although the basic overall dimensions were the same as the other car's, a surprising amount of the work had been done by eye and without measurement. Every joint fitted perfectly; there was no sign anywhere of bodging or second thoughts; where three of four pieces of timber converged into a single joint, they snugged together exactly, each joint being marked by little more than a slight change in colour or gain. As will be seen later, this true sweep of the curves, maybe across several pieces of timber, is vitally important.

Though machine tools such as bandsaws, planers, "thicknessers" which plane to a uniform, given thickness, portable electric drills and suchlike were in use, there is really very little difference between present methods and those used by the old carriage-builders. The machine tools are electric, though, instead of driven from overhead shafts and belting, powered by a single steam engine tucked away in the background. Modern, steel spokeshaves have replaced the wooden ones, in the interests of long life, but

PLATE 44
An original James Young saloon-bodied Rolls-Royce "Twenty" of 1926.

192

the principle is the same; spindle moulders are available, though seldom used; basically, it is the bandsaw, chisel, spokeshave, and to some extent end-mills that form their stock-in-trade.

The body frame completed, it was Terry Hall's turn to take over with the panelling – in 16-gauge aluminium. Eventually, this

PLATE 45
The reproduction body, ash-framed, aluminium-panelled, and indistinguishable from the original.

must fit over the framework, touching the timber everywhere, yet attached to it in very few places indeed, and only by panel pins. If one of Tony's curves is not true, the panelling will follow it faithfully – also untrue, which will show up in the "light-lines". If the radiussed edges of the window frames are not absolutely accurate, the panelling will be inaccurate too, for here it is annealed and then hammered to conform exactly to the timber, and panel-pinned into recesses inside the window slots. It is interesting, here, that between them today's craftsmen were able to improve upon Gurney Nutting's.

On the original body the door panelling stopped at the waistline, the window frames remaining bare wood – to become indistinguishable from the panelling when the paint had been applied. In order to get the glass in and out of the doors, the top rails of the window frames were originally made detachable – with the result that cracks formed at the top, front corners. To avoid this, Tony decided to leave a slot at the top of each door, to be filled by a top-hat section fillet recessed into the top rail. In consequence, they were able to panel the window frames in aluminium and avoid the cracking. Perhaps Gurney Nutting's people would have arrived at this solution, given time.

"You begin with the easy bits", Terry said, "it gives you confidence". This meant the scuttle, panelled in four pieces – from the centreline outwards to the waistline on each side, then downwards from waistline to sills. There is virtually no measuring, except initially to arrive at the approximate size of the individual sections. These are then taken to the wheeling machine – and wheeled and offered-up, wheeled and offered-up until they are an exact fit. Then – and clear of the car, of course, as the timber would be scorched – they are welded together, and offered-up to the scuttle framing. Small adjustments may have to be made until the completed section fits snugly, touching everywhere with the same pressure. Next come the sections between the doors, and the strips that "clad" the A-, B- and C-posts, all these being welded together into an increasingly unwieldy whole. The complicated rear end of the body comes next, from the C-posts behind the rear doors, up over the roof and down to the chassis cross member at the back – always remembering to allow for the turn-over into the door and window recesses where the panel pins will eventually secure it, hidden from sight. There can be no

PLATE 46

The wheeling machine on which panels are shaped – little by little, and by eye alone – until they conform perfectly to the timber frames.

such fastenings on visible panels as they produce a small dent – and may "work" and cause cracks. This rear end panel is made up of a dozen sections, each wheeled and offered-up until it fits – the whole thing being done by eye and feel since it is near-impossible to measure anything so complicated.

Eventually, this vast and unwieldy "body-shell" 'is completed and fitted over the timber frame – an extremely tricky process involving much heaving and shoving, and the use of ropes. Again, this must touch everywhere, for unsupported door panels, for example, will vibrate and crack. All through this panelling process great care must be taken to avoid wheeling the metal too thin in tight, double-radius curves – which is why so many small sections have to be used.

Theoretically, it should be possible to remove the whole thing by pulling out the panel pins and lifting-off. In fact, on this particular body, with a fair amount of "tumble-home" from the waistline downwards to the sills, one final weld was necessary on each side – below the back doors. This is undesirable as, with gas-welding, flux has to be used, and unless this can be cleaned off it will cause corrosion. So a small wedge is cut into the chassis-runner, or lower rail, by Tony, and a metal piece carefully fitted into it, the wedge coinciding with a cut in the panelling. This, then, is welded up, the protecting metal piece removed, the flux cleaned off, and the wooden wedge glued into place to fill the gap. The body-shell is now an exact, precise reproduction of the shape of the frame; it fits exactly, touching firmly everywhere, but with no pressure points or straining. It would in fact remain in position without any fastening.

The panelling process is extremely slow – much slower than the timber framing – which is why there are several examples of Tony's beautiful work stored away in buildings at Church Farm, Ashton Keynes, awaiting Terry's attention with the panelling. There is a $4\frac{1}{2}$-litre Bentley with its aluminium-panelled, open four-seater body covered in leather-cloth – Rexine, American cloth, or whatever it was in the late '20s. There is a vast two-seater body, with long, swept tail, waiting to be panelled and fitted to a Mark VI Bentley chassis – which has had to be lengthened to accommodate it, for it is a replica of a Duesenberg body built for a chassis a foot or more longer than the Bentley's. And there is a charming old Humber two-seater (with "dickey") from the early '20s, its whippy little chassis-frame appreciably stiffened by the bolted-on, timber "chassis runners" that form the basis of the body framework. One appreciates, on looking at this car with all the work that has gone into the framing, how true it is that you can't cut costs just because it isn't a Rolls-Royce. So long as it's a one-off, a coachbuilt body is a coachbuilt body – whatever the chassis.

Is it all worth it – this replica-building, as distinct from true restoration? I think it is – so long as the chassis remains authentic and original, and the present day coachbuilders are doing exactly what their forebears did, using the same methods, materials, tools and design.

What appears at the end of their labours is indistinguishable from the original. But . . . . whose smart, embossed nameplates should appear on the door sills – Gurney Nutting's or Ashton Keynes Vintage Restorations?

19 Harness and Harness Making*

> I would particularly advise that the horse be not
> oppressed with the pinching of the bit, the tightness of
> the harness, nor the too great weight of the carriage . . . .
>
> PHILIP-ASTLEY, 1804

The introduction of harness in about 4000 BC probably marked
man's first effort to control animal power. The first known type
of harness was a yoke, and indeed many of the oxen and asses
were controlled by a ring through the nose; but the horse, from
the start, had a bridle and bit, the latter, in the early days, being
made of bone. By 1400 BC the metal, jointed snaffle bit had arrived,
and from then until 400 BC, when Xenophon mentioned the curb,
it seems that development stopped, as indeed it has for the 23
centuries which followed.

The origins of leather as a suitable material for harness are
even vaguer than those of the actual harness, but Egyptian carvings show leather dressers at work, and Pliny comments on the
use of bark and berries as tanning ingredients, so it would be
reasonable to suppose that leather was in use from the start. It
has remained so ever since, for reasons inherent in its nature. A
blend of strength, flexibility and durability makes leather ideal
for the manufacture of "modern" harness, which first appeared on
frescoes in Hanso, China, in 500 AD and then slowly travelled
west to Europe by 800 AD. Prior to these dates, harness had been
unsatisfactory, because it put too much pressure on the jugular
vein and windpipe. The changes moved the strain on to the
shoulders, and enabled the animal to throw all its weight against
the load. Our European forbears would probably look down
upon the English harness, so popular through the years, as
it has traditionally always been lighter than its Continental
counterpart.

Nevertheless, England has always been in the forefront of the
development of horse transport, and its harness makers have been
held in high regard up to the present day.

*See Introduction.

The production of leather for harness and saddle is still very laborious and although new materials and techniques are constantly being introduced, it is still a task better suited to the small unit than the large mass-production one. The very best hides have to be selected from the world's markets and then fastidiously processed so that the end-product has the correct feel, appearance and durability. It must be mellow but not soft, firm but not hard; it must have just the right amount of grease for it to resist water without feeling too slippery, or swelling; and to do this the amount of time, heat and quantity of ingredients applied must be regulated minutely. As an example, too cold a drum, in which the harness backs are tumbled with the stuffing grease (usually a mixture of tallow and cod oil), and the leather will not absorb properly; too hot and the grease will not stay in the fibres and the hides will "burn" in the drum.

One of the leading leather-dressers for nearly 100 years has had a long and close association with the Coachmakers' and Coach Harness Makers' Company, namely Connolly Brothers, seven of whose family members spread through three generations and include two Masters. A look through their specification books reveals some of the age old ingredients that are still used, like oakbark, tallow, cod oil, whale oil, linseed and mineral oil dubbin. The terms used to describe various processes seem to have their origin back in history; canking, samming, staining, stuffing, skiving, shaving, jacking and sleaking, roll easily off the tongue and conjure up images of warehouses hung with hides and lined with the giant revolving drums in which the hides are prepared. Modern methods have, at last, improved the working conditions of tanners and curriers, though hides are still heavy, particularly when wet and until someone breeds cows of uniform shape, a lot of the handling will have literally to be manual.

The trade of harness making passed through a lean period from the 1920s with the decline in the commercial use of the horse. By the end of the Great War, the car had replaced the horse not only as an instrument of work, but also to a lesser extent as a vehicle of pleasure. Some of the few changes that have affected harness, such as increases in weight, have been caused by wars, which also cause surges in levels of production; there are the cutbacks which inevitably follow the end of a war.

In the 1920s many famous harness making names disappeared, and many craftsmen were lost, leaving only a few, trapped by age or a genuine love for their trade, to split up the sadly diminished business. It needs only a gap of three or four generations and a vital part of an art can disappear for ever. Most craftsmen, with a pride in their specialised skills, can be coaxed into passing on what they know. What they are not consciously aware they know is the very heart of their individual knowledge. Over the years experience teaches them to make an adjustment to the regular technique – to stitch stronger there, be gentler here. They learn, subconsciously, to make allowances when staining a hide for a variation in grain; when cutting a hide they will vary the length to compensate for a difference in dressing. It is these techniques, assimilated rather than consciously learned, that they do not think to pass on when asked. How can they when they're not consciously aware of what they know? Yet this is the essence of the trade; and where the trade is one which uses natural materials

PLATE 47

According to the description accompanying this print published by R. Ackermann, the harness shown on the horses was for a "curriacle" and a phaeton. The postillion holding them, whip tucked in the top of his boot, is wearing the beaver hat in which he was traditionally believed to carry all his belongings.

199

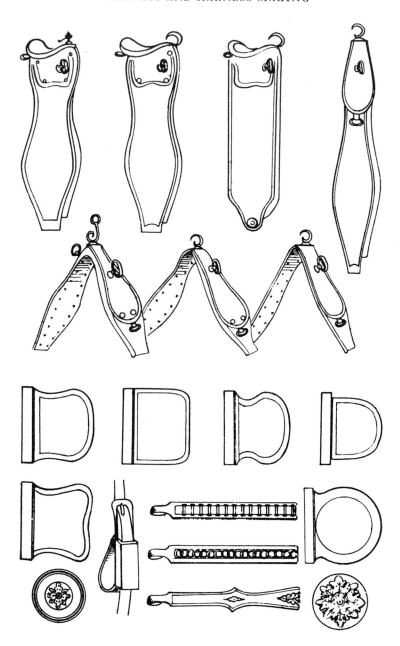

PLATE 48

Patterns of various harness items. At the top are gig saddles; in the centre, pads for four-in-hand and pair-horse vehicles; below, various blinkers, brow bands and rosettes.

like wood or leather, in which variations of grain are inevitable and welcome, then these are the lifeblood which *must* be passed on.

England has been lucky, through the years of mechanical transport, that reputation and strong sporting links have brought just enough continuity to ensure that leather working skills have not been forgotten, though there is a shortage of skilled men. Conditions improved in the 1970s. With the renewed interest in riding and driving the volume of business in the saddlery and harness trade grew internationally from £12½ million in 1972 to about £25 million in 1974 and continued to rise in successive years in England. The old established London firm of W. & H. Gidden, one of the few still capable of making "four-in-hand" harness, a set of which costs over £2,000, regularly export sets of single harness to Austria, Australia, Germany, Sweden, the Middle East, U.S.A. and Holland. Single harness cost over £500 a set in 1976; the 1939 price was £15 – £25. For comparison, the coachbuilder for a family coach submitted this inclusive estimate in 1740:

> To four new harness made with the best neats leather, a brass plate on the edge of housing crest, housing plates, brass watering hooks, starrs, and screwed rings to ye head stalls, double bard bits, and a sett of reins, £12.

Furniture is a name applied to the foundations and mountings of harness which include the hames, terrets, rings, buckles &c. There were some 12 or 14 varieties of harness mountings in use. Silver-plating in its different forms was by far the most widely used.

Harness making is again enjoying a time of considerable demand at home and overseas.

Appendix A:
The Charter of King Charles II

King Charles II's Charter to the Company was granted on the 31st May, 1677. Like all such charters, it is written without a break from beginning to end and is without punctuation. Indication of separate subjects dealt with is made by the use of words in capital letters. For convenience in reading, the Charter has been paragraphed. Otherwise the text below is a careful copy, made from the original vellum. The very few contractions used have been filled out, and in places the sign "j" has been substituted for the "i" of early use.

CHARLES THE SECOND BY THE GRACE OF GOD KING of England Scotland France and Ireland Defender of the Faith &c TO ALL TO WHOM THESE PRESENTS SHALL COME

WHEREAS Wee have byn informed by the humble Peticion of many of our well beloved subjects the Coach makers and Coach Harness makers within our Cittyes of London and Westminster that their Arts Trades and Misteries are of antiquity and great use and beneficiall to the Noblemen of our Kingdom and other our Subjects

AND that in their Arts and Misteries there is not only required skill and good workmanshipp but also great care and trust in provideing and useing good and proper materialls

AND that the said Trades Arts and Misteries have great Dependences each with other and cannot conveniently be exercised and followed without good Rule Order and Government among them And that noe one perticuler Trade save only such as exercise and follow the Arts Trades and Misteries of makeing fitting finishing and selling of Coaches and Coach Harnesse have knowledge and skill in All the workes workemanshipps and materialls used in the same Arts and Trades nor how to discover or find out the abuses therein practised And that divers unexpert and unskilfull persons inhabiting within the said Cittyes and other parts neare adjacent unto the same have of late intruded into the said Trades and Misteries not haveing served up theire Apprenticeshipps nor byn trained up in any of the said Trades or Misteries and for want of due knowledge and skill or else by fraud and deceit in their Materialls and Workmanshipp have abused and do daily abuse many of our Noblemen and others our subjects to theire very great losse and

202

dammage and to the discreditt abuse and disparagement of all skilfull and honest Artificers lawfull using the said Arts and Misteries

THEREFORE they have humbly besought us that Wee would bee graciously pleased to incorporate them and all others that now lawfully use and exercise the said Trades or Misteries within our said Cittyes of London and Westminster and the Libertyes thereof and within twenty miles distante from the same into a Body Pollitique and Corporatte and to invest them with power and jurisdiction for the well ordering and governing the said Trades Arts and Misteries and all such as use and shall use or exercise the same within the said Cittyes and lymitts aforesaid And wee minding the welfare of our said subjects and intending to restraine and suppresse idle and unskilfull persons intruders into the said Trades or Misteries or either of them and to appropriate them to such person and persons as heretofore have beene or hereafter shall bee orderly and honestly educated and brought up as Apprentices therein according to the Lawes of this our Realme in that behalfe made and provided And the better to avoyd for the future all deceipts and abuses as are used or practised in the said Trades and Manufactures to the end there may bee better Order and Government established and kept among the persons useing the said Trades and Misteries And for the due encouragement of such as are or shall bee honestly bred upp and serve their Apprenticeshipps in any of the said Trades or Manufactures and for the suppressing and restreyning of such unskillful persons as shall unduely presume or attempt to practise any of the said Trades or Misteries

NOW KNOW YE that Wee being alwaies graciously enclyned to the humble suits of our Subjects and especially in those things which tend to the common good and benefit and for divers other good Causes and considerations Wee hereunto especially moving of our especiall grace, certaine knowledge and meere mocion

HAVE willed ordeyned constituted declared and granted And by these Presents for us our heirs and Successors Do will declare constitute ordeyne and grant That our well beloved Subjects William Bussey James Masters James Page Stephen Phillips Edmund Awbry our Coachmaker Charles Nevill our Coach Harnesse maker Thomas Brigham Coachmaker to Our Dear Brother the Duke of York Richard Halbert Edward Hooper John Davies John Parsons Clement Ryter James Blagrave Robert Johnson William Fowler Zachariah Taylor William Parrott John Hunt Jacob Smith Richard Taylor Thomas London William Rose Nicholas Rowse Benjamin Thody ffrancis Carey John Read John Darker James Waters Thomas Riland Thomas Templeman Thomas Phelps George Barrett Edward Knight John Crosse William Watson George Burton Henry Birle James Tremblett

William Morgan Robert Wilmott Thomas Perkins William Cope Richard Thody Henry Welch Samuell Miller Nicholas Kempe Richard Rowse John Brigham Richard Brigham Edward Lindsey Walter Bingley Thomas Fox Thomas Newcombe Lawrence Wright Jacob Terrett Isaac Terrett Richard Torlington James Elson Jonathan Bentley Thomas Austin Richard Pryor Edward Phillips Edmund Callow Thomas Ricks Joseph Hewett John Clarke John Man Edward Cooke Philip Davis John Howell Richard Pearce William Bassett John Bradford Edward Salisbury Norris Salisbury Henry Bland Thomas Crowley John Rowlitt Ralph Major Richard Hobbs and William Dancer and all others that now professe the said Trades Arts or Misteries of a Coachmaker or a Coach Harnesse maker or that sell utter make or finish any Coaches Chariotts or Coach Harnesse or any of them and have used the same Trades Arts or Misteries or any of them by the space of seaven yeares as Apprentices within our said Citties of London or Westminster or in the Suburbs or Libertyes thereof or in the Burrough of Southwarke or in any of the Burroughs Parishes Townes Villages Hamletts or Places whatsoever within twenty miles distant from the said Citties or either of them and all others that shall hereafter use or exercise the same Trades Arts or Misteries or either of them and shall have served as Apprentices thereunto within the places and lymitts aforesaid by the space of seaven yeares att least shall bee from henceforth for ever hereafter One Body pollitique and Corporate in Deed and in Name by the name of the Master Wardens Assistants and Commonalty of the Company of Coachmakers and Coach Harnesse makers of London And them by the name of Master Wardens Assistants and Commonalty of the Company of Coachmakers and Coach Harnesse makers of London one body pollitique and corporate

WE DO for us our heires and Successors fully absolutely and really erect create Constitute ordeyne Declare make and establish by these Presents And that by the same name of Master Wardens Assistants and Commonalty of the Company of Coachmakers and Coach Harnesse makers of London they shall have perpetuall succession and contynuance for ever And that they and their successors by the said name of Master Wardens Assistants and Commonalty of the Company of Coachmakers and Coach Harnesse makers of London shall bee for ever hereafter persons able and capable in the Law to have take purchase hold receive possesse and enjoy as well any Mannors Messuages Lands Tenements Libertyes Priviledges Jurisdictions ffranchises Rents Reversions and other Hereditaments whatsoever of what kind nature or Quality soever that bee to them and their successors in ffee and Perpetuity or for terme of life lives yeares or otherwise in what sort soever not exceeding the yearely value of Three Hundred Pounds of lawful money of England per annu besides the Hall for theire meeting hereinafter mentioned As also all manner of Goods Chattels and Things Personall of what kind or sort soever and of what value soever they bee without suing forth any writt or writts of ad quod dampnum

AND NOTWITHSTANDING the Statute of not putting Lands and Tenements into mortmaine or any other Statute Act Ordinance or Provision heretofore had made ordayned or provided or any other cause matter or thing whatsoever to the contrary thereof in any wise notwithstanding.

AND ALSO Give grant Demise lett aliene Assigne sett over and dispose of all or any the said Mannors Messuages Lands Tenements and Hereditaments Goods and Chattells at their will and pleasure to any Person or Persons whatsoever and to make seale and accomplish all Deeds Evidences and Writings of for or concerning the same or any part thereof And likewise to doe and Execute all and singuler other Acts and things whatsoever by the name aforesaid And by the same name of the Master Wardens Assistants and Commonalty of the Company of Coachmakers and Coach Harness makers of London they and their Successors shall and may bee persons able and capable in Law to plead and bee impleaded to answeare and be answeared unto to defend and bee defended in what Court or Courts soever and before any Judge or Justices or other persons and Officers whomsoever of us our heirs and Successors in all and singular Actions Pleas Causes Suits matters and demands of what kind Quality or sort soever And also to doe performe and execute all such Acts and things whatsoever in the same and in as ample manner and forme as any other of our loveing people and subjects of this our Realme of England being persons able and capable in the Law or any other Corporation Body Politique or Corporate within this realm of England can or may have purchase receive possesse enjoy retayne give grant lett aliene dispose and Assign plead and bee impleaded answeare and be answeared unto defend and be defended doe performe and execute by any lawfull waies or meanes whatsoever And that the said Master Wardens Assistants and Commonalty of the Company of Coach makers and Coach Harnesse makers and theire Successors shall and may for ever hereafter have a Common Seale for the ensealing doeing and confirming of all and singular the Causes affaires matters and businesse touching or concerning the said Company And that it shall and may be lawful to and for the Master Wardens and Assistants of the said Company of Coachmakers and Coach Harnesse makers of London or their Successors for the tyme being or the greater Number of them to breake alter and make new the said Seale from tyme to tyme at theire wills and pleasures when and as often as they shall thinke fitt

AND FURTHER WEE WILL and for us our heirs and successors doe grant and Ordeyne by these Presents that from henceforth for ever hereafter there shall be one Master three Wardens and three and Twenty Assistants of the said Company of Coachmakers and Coach Harnesse makers of London to bee constituted and chosen in such manner and forme as hereafter in these Presents is expressed and specified And for the better Executing of this our grant intent and meaning in that behalfe and for the good Rule and Government of the said Company of Coachmakers and Coach Harnesse makers of London from tyme to tyme for ever

WEE HAVE ASSIGNED and ordeyned and constituted And by these Presents for us and our heires and successors DO ASSIGNE Name Ordayne and Constitute our welbeloved Subject William Bussey to bee first and present Master of the said Company of Coachmakers and Coach Harnesse makers of London to contynue in the said Office from the day of the date of these Presents unto the first day of September which shall bee in the yeare of our Lord One thousand six hundred Seventy and Eight if hee shall soe long live or shall not bee in that tyme removed for some just and reasonable cause And from thenceforth untill one other of the said Company shall bee chosen and sworne into the said Office of Master in due manner according to the Ordinances and provisions in this behalfe in these Presents mentioned and expressed hee the said William Bussey taking his Corporall Oath upon the Holy Evangelists before the Lord Mayor or the Recorder of London for the tyme being or one of the Masters of our High Court of Chancery for the due and faithfull Execution of the said Office of Master Which Lord Mayor of London Recorder or Master of our High Court of Chancery or any one of them Wee doe hereby Authorize to administer and give the said Oath unto the said William Bussey accordingly

AND ALSO WEE HAVE ASSIGNED named ordeyned constituted And by these Presents for us our heirs and Successors DOE ASSIGNE name Ordeyne and constitute our welbeloved subjects James Masters James Page and Stephen Phillips to be the first three and present Wardens of the said Company of Coachmakers and Coach Harnesse makers of London to contynue in their said Offices from the date of these Presents unto the first day of September which shall be in the year of our Lord One thousand six hundred seventy and eight if they shall soe long live or shall not before that tyme bee removed for some just and reasonable cause and from thenceforth untill some other meete and sufficient persons of the said Company of Coachmakers and

Coach Harnesse makers of London bee to the said Offices of Wardens duly elected and sworn to Execute the same according to these Presents or the Ordinances or Provisions herein after Lymited and expressed They the said Wardens severally takeing theire Corporall Oathes before the Master of the said Company then being or before one of the Masters of our High Court of Chancery for the due performance of the said Places of Wardens

AND WEE DO hereby authorize any one of the Masters of our High Court of Chancery or the Master of the said Company or any of them to administer and give the said Oathes to the said Wardens respectively And so ever after the Wardens of the said Company for the tyme being to take their Oathes before the Master of the said Company for the tyme being to whom Wee doe hereby give full power and authority to administer the same

AND MOREOVER for the better ayding and assisting of the Master and Wardens of the said Company for the tyme being in all affairs matters and things touching the said Company and the good government thereof

WEE LIKEWISE HAVE ASSIGNED constituted made and appointed And by these Presents for us our heires and successors DOE ASSIGNE name constitute make and appoint the said Edmund Aubry our Coachmaker Charles Nevill our Coach Harnesse maker Thomas Brigham Coachmaker to our deare Brother the Duke of York Richard Halbert Edward Hooper John Davis John Parsons Clement Ryter James Blagrave Robert Johnson William ffowler Zachariah Taylor William Parrott John Hunt Jacob Smith Richard Taylor Thomas London William Rose Nicholas Rowse Benjamyne Thody ffrancis Carey John Read and John Darker to be the first and present Assistants of the said Company of Coachmakers and Coach Harnesse makers of London to continue in the said Offices and Places of Assistants during their naturall lives unlesse the said number shall bee thought fitt to be contracted by the Master Wardens and Assistants of the said Company for the tyme being or by the major part of them according to the power hereby given them or that they or any of them for just and reasonable cause shall bee thence removed who are from tyme to tyme to be ayding councelling and assisting unto the Master and Wardens of the said Company for the tyme being in all things for the better Rule government and direction of the said Master Wardens and Company and every Member thereof and for the makeing and establishing good reasonable and wholesome Orders Statue Acts and Ordinances for the well order and Government of the said Company and every member thereof They the said Assistants takeing their several corporall oathes before the Master and Wardens of the said Company for the tyme being or any two of them for the due and faithful execution of the said places of Assistants Which said Master and Wardens or any two of them as aforesaid Wee doe hereby for us our heires and successors authorize and appoint to administer the said Oaths from tyme to tyme accordingly And so for ever after the persons to be bee elected to the place of Assistant to take their corporall Oaths before the Master and Wardens of the said Company for the tyme being or any two of them as aforesaid

AND FURTHER WEE WILL and by these Presents for us our heires and successors DOE ordeyne and grant unto the said Master Wardens Assistants and Commonalty of the said Company of Coachmakers and Coach Harnesse makers of London and their Successors that the Election of the Masters and Wardens of the said Company shall bee made on the first day of September yearely for ever unlesse the same happen to bee a Sunday and then on the Munday next ensuing in manner following that is to say the Master Wardens and Assistants of the said Company of Coachmakers and Coach Harnesse makers of London for the tyme being or the greatest part of them being then assembled att or in some House or Hall to be by them and for theire use provided within the said Citty of London or the Suburbs or Liberties thereof To whome wee do hereby for us our heires and Successors give full power Lycence and Authority to purchase the same shall Nominate elect and chuse a fitt and sufficient Person who hath byn formerly one of the Wardens or is an Assistant of the said Company to be Master of the said Company for the yeare ensueing as aforesaid And soe the Master to bee every yeare Annually Elected and Chosen unto the Office of Master upon the said ffirst day of September if it bee not a Sunday or if Sunday then the day next ensuing and soe from thence to contynue one whole yeare then next following or untill some other shall bee elected into the said Office by reason of such Death or removall as aforesaid

AND WEE WILL and Grant that the Master Wardens and Assistants for the tyme being or the greatest part of them from and after the said first day of September which shall be in the year of our Lord One thousand six hundred seveanty and eight shall and may yearely and every yeare on the first day of September if itt bee not Sunday or if itt bee Sunday then the next day att their Hall or place of meeting and assembly as aforesaid Nominate Elect and chuse out of the Assistants Three that shall be Wardens of the said Company Which said Wardens so as aforesaid to be Nominated Elected and Chosen shall bee and contynue Wardens of the said Company untill the end and terme of one whole yeare then next ensuing and from thence untill some other meete persons shall be chosen and sworn unto the said Office of Wardens in manner aforesaid if the same Wardens shall soe long live or shall not bee removed thence for just and reasonable causes as aforesaid They the said Master and Wardens soe newly elected and chosen and every of them respectively first takeing a Corporall Oath upon the holy Evangelists before the last Master and Wardens or any two of them for the due execution of the severall Offices and Places To whom Wee doe hereby give full power to administer the said oathes And then every such Master and Wardens soe from tyme to tyme leaving and departing from his or their said Places of Master and Wardens respectively as aforesaid (unless removed from theire said places for some just and reasonable Causes as aforesaid) shall then instantly become and remaine an Assistant and Assistants of the said Company in the roome or Place of him or them that shalbe soe chosen out of the Assistants to bee Master and Wardens of the said Company as aforesaid They first takeing their Corporall Oathes for the due performance of the office and place of Assistants as aforesaid if they have not byn before Chosen out thereout and sworne before he and they take upon them the Execution of the said Place of an Assistant or Assistants

AND FURTHER by these Presents We for us our heires and Successors Do Will and Grant unto the Masters Wardens Assistants and Commonalty of the said Company and theire Successors That if itt shall happen that the Master and Wardens of the said Company for the tyme being or any one of them at any time within one yeare after that they or any of them bee Chosen into his or their office or offices do dye or be removed from his or their said office or offices or for some just or reasonable cause (which said Master and Wardens or any of them for just and reasonable cause Wee Will shall bee from tyme to tyme removable by the Master Wardens and Assistants or the greater Number of them for the tyme being being assembled as aforesaid) That then and soe often itt shall be lawfull to and for such and soe many of the Masters Wardens and Assistants which shalbe then liveing or remayneing or the greater part of them att their Wills and pleasures to Chuse make and sweare one or more other or others of the Wardens or Assistants for the tyme being to bee Master Warden or Wardens of the said Company according to the Orders and Provisions in these Presents expressed and declared to Execute and Exercise the said Office or Offices of Master or of Warden or Wardens of the said Company untill the said ffirst day of September then next following and from thence untill a New Election bee made in manner aforesaid into the said Office or Offices of Master or of Warden or Wardens of the said Company hee or they ffirst takeing his or their corporall oath or oathes in forme as aforesaid and soe as often as the case shall require

AND FURTHER WEE WILL and by these Presents for us our heires and Successors DOE graunt unto the said Master Wardens Assistants and Commonalty of the said Company of Coachmakers and Coach Harnesse makers of London and their successors that whensoever itt shall happen any of the Assistants of the said Company for the tyme being to dye or bee removed from his or their Office or Offices Place or Places of Assistant or Assistants (which Assistant and every or any of them WE WILL shall be removeable or removed by the greater part of the Master Wardens and Assistants for the tyme being for evill Government or misbehaviour or for any other just and reasonable Cause) That then and so often itt shall and may bee lawful to and for the Master Wardens and Assistants for the tyme being of the said Company which shall then survive and remaine or the greater part of them att their Wills and pleasures from tyme to tyme to choose and name one other or more of the Commonalty of the said Company to bee Assistant or Assistants of the said Company in his or their Place or stead who shall soe happen to dye or be removed as aforesaid And that he or they after that he or they shall be so named or chosen to bee Assistant or Assistants of the said Company as aforesaid before that he or they or any of them bee Admitted to the execution of the said office of Assistant or Assistants shall take his and theire corporall oath or oathes well and truly to execute the said Office before the Master and Wardens of the said Company or any three of them To whom Wee doe hereby give full power and Authority to Administer the said oathes accordingly

AND FURTHER WEE WILL and by these Presents for us our heires and Successors DOE graunt unto the said Master Wardens Assistants and Commonalty of the said Company and their Successors That they and theire Successors shall and may have one honest and discreet Person in manner hereafter in these Presents expressed to be Chosen and named which shall bee and shalbe called Clerke of the said Company And one or more Person or Persons which shall be and shalbe called the Beadle or Beadles of the said Company And that from tyme to tyme the said Master Wardens and Assistants of the said Company or the greater number of them shall and may chuse and name the Person or Persons to be Clerke or Beadle or Beadles of the said Company for the tyme being And that hee and they shalbe so chosen Clerke or Beadle or Beadles of the same Company shall and may exercise the said offices of Clerke or Beadle or Beadles of the said Company respectively whereunto hee or they shalbe chosen during the good will and pleasure of the Master Wardens and Assistants of the said Company or the greater part of them every Clerke or Beadle or Beadles of the said Company to be elected and chosen as aforesaid ffirst taking his and their corporall oath and oathes before the Master Wardens and

Assistants of the said Company for the tyme being or any five or more
of them to whom We doe give power to Administer the said Oath and
Oathes well and truly to execute such Office or Offices whereunto hee
or they shalbe so Elected or Chosen according to his and their best
skill and knowledge And soe from tyme to tyme as often as the Cases
shalbe need or require

AND OF OUR further especiall grace certain knowledge and meere
mocion WE WILL and by these Presents for us our heires and
Successors Doe graunt to the said Master Wardens Assistants and
Commonalty of the said Company and their Successors for ever that it
shall and may bee lawfull to and for the Master Wardens and Assistants
of the said Company for the tyme being and their successors or the
greater Number of them when and as often as itt shall seeme needfull
or expedient to Assemble convocate and congregate themselves
together att or in theire Hall or Place of meeting And there from tyme
to tyme and at all tymes convenient hereafter to Treate Consult
Determine Ordain and make any Constitutions Statutes Laws
Ordinances Articles and Orders whatsoever which to them or the
greater number of them shall seem reasonable profitable or requisite
for touching or concerning the good Estate Rule or Government of the
said Masters Wardens Assistants and Commonalty of the said
Company and every member thereof And in what order and manner
the said Master Wardens and Assistants of the said Company and their
successors shall demeane and behave themselves as well in all and
singular matters Causes and thing touching or concerning the said
Arts Trades or Misteries of a Coachmaker and Coach Harnesse maker
or either of them as alsoe in theire severall Offices ffunctions misteries
and buisnesses touching or concerning the said Company as aforesaid
Any reasonable ffines paines penalties and fforfeitures to impose and
sett from tyme to tyme upon the offenders against such Lawes
Ordinances and Orders respectively And all and singular such ffines
paines penalties and fforfeitures soe to bee sett and imposed upon any
such Offender or Offenders which shall transgresse breake or violate
the said Constitutions Lawes Oathes Statutes Articles or Ordinances
to bee made ordeyned and established as aforesaid or any of them
To Ask Recover Leavy take and receive by Action of Debt or by way
of Distresse or by any other lawfull wayes or meanes of or against the
Offender or Offenders his or theire Bodies or Chattels or any of them
as the Case shall require And as to the Master Wardens and Assistants
of the said Company for the tyme being or the greater number of them
shall seeme meete and expedient All which Laws Ordinances
Constitutions Orders and Articles soe to bee made ordeyned or
Established and every of them WEE WILL and by these Presents for

us and our heirs and Successors DOE Grant and Command to bee from tyme to tyme and at all tymes observed obeyed and performed in all things as the same ought to bee under the reasonable amerciaments penalties and fforfeitures in the same to be provided or Lymitted soe as the same Lawes Statutes Oathes Articles Ordinances Orders paines penalties and amerciaments or any of them bee not repugnant or contrary but as neere as may be agreeable to the Lawes and Statutes of this our Realme of England and not prejudiciall to the Customes of the Citty of London

AND WHEREAS it is found that many unexpert and unskilful and fraudulent persons have and do dayly assume and take upon them the said Arts Trades and Misteries of a Coachmaker and Coach Harnesse maker who therein have committed many abuses

WEE minding to provide and for the Reformation thereof DOE hereby for our heirs and successors streightly Charge and Command that noe person or persons whatsoever other than the said Master Wardens Assistants and Commonalty and their Successors and such as shall from tyme to tyme be free of the said Company and shall have served as an Apprentice or Apprentices with some Person or Persons which are or shalbe free of the said Company by the space of seaven yeares at least shall att any tyme hereafter within our said Citties of London and Westminster or the Suburbs or Liberties thereof or within any Burrough Parish Hamlett Village or Place or Places whatsoever within Twenty Miles distant from the same Citties or either of them shall or may use exercise or follow the said Trades Arts or Misteries of a Coachmaker or Coach harnessmaker upon such paines penalties and punishments as by the Lawes and Statutes of this Realme can or may bee lawfully inflicted on such Offender or Offenders for his or theire Contempt or neglect of our Royall Will and pleasure herein declared And for the better discovery of all abuses and deceits or inartificiall workemanshippe now practised or that hereafter may bee practised in the said Trades Arts or Misteries of a Coachmaker or Coach harnessmaker or either of them or in anything thereunto appertaineing

WEE DOE by these presents for us our heirs and successors give and Graunt full power and Authority to the Master Wardens and Assistants of the said Company for the tyme being or any three or more of them whereof the Master or one of the Wardens to bee always one such meete and skilfull person or persons of the said Company as the Master Wardens and Assistants of the said Company or the greater Number of them for the tyme being under the Common seale of the said Company shall Depute Name or Assigne having obteined a Warrant from the Lord Chiefe Justice of the Kings Bench for the tyme being in that behalfe with a Constable or other Lawfull Officer in the day time only to enter into any Shopps Cellars Sollars Stables Coachhouses or other suspected place within our Cities of London and Westminster and the Liberties and Suburbs thereof and in all Burroughs Parrishes Villages Hamletts and Places within Twenty miles Compas or any way distant from the said Citties or either of them There to view Search and Examine all or any Coaches Chariotts Coach Harnesse and the fitting Trimming Working materialls and workemanship thereof and to search for and find out all and every misdemeaners defects and deceitfull Works and materialls To this end that due and legall course and prosecution may bee had and taken against all and every such Offender or Offenders And to prosecute and punish all and every Offender and Offenders according to due Course of Law And to the end that from tyme to tyme all the members of the said Company that shall practise or use the said Trades Arts or Misteries of a Coachmaker or Coach Harnesse maker in the said Citties of London and Westminster Burrough of Southwarke and within Twenty miles compas or any way distant from the same Citties or either of them may become ffree Coachmakers and Coach Harnesse makers in Deed and in Name of the City of London and free of the same Company alsoe and soe be brought under better Government than otherwise they would be

OUR WILL and pleasure is AND WEE DOE streightly Charge and Command And by these Presents for us our heirs and successors DOE graunt unto the said Masters Wardens and Assistants and Commonalty and their Successors That all such Apprentices as hereafter any Coachmaker or Coach Harnesse maker of London or any others being members of the said Company and using the said Arts Misteries or Trades of a Coachmaker or Coach Harnesse maker within the lymitts or compasse of Twenty miles distant from the same as aforesaid shall take into his or theire Service shalbe bound Apprentices to a Coachmaker or Coach Harnesse maker free of the Citty of London and of the said Company and such Apprentices to bee presented according to the Ordinances of the said Company in that behalfe to bee made and provided upon paine that every person who shall bind his Apprentice or Apprentices in other manner or shall have or bind more in number att a time then by the Ordnances of the said Company shalbe lymitted shall fforfeite and pay such ffine and sumes of money to the use and benefit of the said Company for every such Offence as by such Ordinances shalbe reasonably sett and imposed in that behalfe and to bee recovered in cases of denyall of payment by Action of Debt or by Distresse for the same in the same or like manner as for other ffines and penalties aforesaid

AND OUR WILL and pleasure is that All Mayors Sherriffs Justices of the Peace Chamberlayns and all other Officers whom the same doth or may concern shall take care thereof and see this our Royall Will and pleasure to be Executed and performed herein and to permitt and suffer this our Royall graunt to be introlled in the City of London in such Places and Courts as our Charters or Letters Patente in such cases are used to bee enrolled on paine of our displeasure

AND FURTHER of our especiall grace certaine knowledge and meere mocion WEE HAVE given and graunted And by these Presents for us and our heirs and Successors DOE give and graunt unto the said Master Wardens Assistants and Commonalty and theire Successors speciall Lycensse power and Authority to have Purchase Receive and Take to them and their Successors in ffee Simple or for terme of Life Lives or for yeares or otherwise howsoever Mannors Messuages Meadows ffeedings Pastures Woods Underwoods Rectories Tythes Rentes Revercons and other Hereditaments whatsoever within this our Realme of England or elsewhere within any our Dominions as well as of us our heirs and Successors as of any other Person or Persons so as the said Mannors Messuages Lands Tenements Meadows ffeedings Pastures Woods Underwoods Rectories Tythes Rentes Revercons Services and other Hereditaments do not exceed in the whole the cleere yearely value of Three Hundred pounds of Lawful mones of England by the yeare above all Charges and Reprizes besides their Comon Hall or Place for theire Assembling together about the publick matters and Government of the said Company above mentioned without sueing forth of any Writt or Writts of ad quod dampnum

AND NOTWITHSTANDING the Statute of Not putting Lands and Tenements into mortmaine or any other Statute Act Ordinance or Provision heretofore had made Ordeined or Provided or any other thing Cause or matter whatsoever to the contrary thereof in anywise notwithstanding

AND WEE DOE hereby for us our heirs and Successors give and Grant lycence and Authority to all or any of our Subjects to give Graunt Bargain Sell Devise and Bequeath unto the said Master Wardens Assistants and Commonalty and their Successors Mannors Messuages Lands Tenements and Hereditaments of such yearely value and in such manner as aforesaid

AND WE FURTHER WILL and by these Presents for us our heirs and successors doe streightly Charge and Command the Lord Mayor of our Citty of London and all other Officers and Ministers within our said Citties of London and Westminster and either of them for the tyme being And all and singular other Mayors Sheriffs Justices of Peace Constables Bayliffs Headboroughs and other Officers of us our heirs and Successors whatsoever in all and every place and places whatsoever as well exempt and privileged as not excempt and privileged within our Citties of London and Westminster and the Suburbs and Liberties thereof and within Twenty miles distant of the same that they and every of them att all and every tyme and.tymes hereafter and from tyme to tyme upon reasonable request to them or any of them to be made in that behalfe to be furthering Ayding Helping and Assisting to the said Master Wardens Assistants and Commonalty of the said Company for the tyme being and every or any of them And to such person or persons as shall from tyme to tyme bee under the Comon Seale of the said Company Deputed or Assigned as aforesaid as well for and in the execution of these our Letters Patente as of all and singular lawful and reasonable Ordinances Lawes Constitutions and Orders hereafter by virtue of these Presents to bee by them made which shalbe allowed and approved of according to the Lawes and Statutes of this our Realme and for the doeing executing and performing of all and singular the Premisses according to the tenur of these Presents

PROVIDED ALLWAYES and our Will and pleasure is and by these Presents for us our Heirs and Successors WEE DOE streightly Charge and Comand That the said Master Wardens and Assistants in and by these our Letters Patente Constituted and appointed or by virtue hereof to bee Constituted and appointed shall before they bee admitted into theire severall and respective Offices and places take the Oath of Allegiance upon the holy Evangelists before such Person or Persons as by the Lawes and Statutes of this our Realme of England are att present designed or appointed or hereafter shalbe Designed and appointed to give and Administer the same

IN WITNESS whereof we have caused these our Letters to be made Patente Witness our self att Westminster the one and Thirtieth day of May in the Nine and Twentieth year of our Reign

By Writt of Privy Seal
PIGOTT

	li	s	d
pro fine	xiij	vj	viij

FINCH C.

Appendix B:
Masters and Clerks of the Company

Election Day is 1st September and the year given for each name, unless otherwise stated, is from 1st September in each year until 31st August of the year following. The 1st September is the feast of St. Egidius, whom we call St. Giles; there seems no particular association between him and the craft which ultimately became coach-making.

MASTERS

1677	William Bussey (named in first charter)	1698	Thomas Kirkham
1678	James Masters	1699	James Trumble
1679	James Page (named on Poorbox)	1700	Isaac Territt
1680	Stephen Phillips	1701 / 1702	Jonathan Bentley
1681	Charles Nevill	1703	Edward Salisbury
1682	Edward Hooper	1704	Norwich Salisbury
1683	John Davis	1705	Thomas Walker
1684	John Parsons	1706	Josiah Linnet (died May, 1707)
1685	Robert Johnson	——	Jonathan Bentley
1686	William Fowler	1707	Samuel Browne
1687	Benjamin Thody	1708 / 1709	John Parsons
1688	John Bradford (named in second charter)	1710	Richard Cheshire
——	William Fowler	1711	Joseph Parsons
1689	William Perrott	1712	Joseph Shefford
1690	John Hunt	1713	Isaac Territt
1691	Jacob Smith	1714	William King
1692	Richard Taylor	1715	John Edmonds
1693	William Rose	1716	Joseph Bernard
1694	John Darker, jun.	1717	Joseph Jacob
1695	Nicholas Spalden	1718	William Beaumont
1696	Richard Atkinson (died April, 1697)	1719	Francis Maskull
——	Benjamin Thody	1720	John King
1697	William Dancer	1721	Richard Hipwell
		1722	Henry Glover

1723	Thomas Burgiss	1759	Benjamin Lancaster
1724	James Price	1760	John Virgoe
1725	Charles Haman	1761	William Goodenough
1726	Joseph Barnard (died January, 1727)	1762	Richard Payne
		1763	George Austen
——	Thomas Burgiss	1764	William Piddington
1727	Robert Grimes	1765	Shadrach Venden
1728	Thomas Smithsend	1766	John Westley
1729	John Jatt	1767	John Wright
1730	Richard White	1768	Samuel Butler
1731	William Neaton	1769	John Orme
1732	Benjamin Nolton	1770	Richard Spencer
1733	Thomas Sells	1771	James Cope
1734	William Thorp	1772	Justus Olney
1735	Edward Salisbury	1773	Henry Sturdy
1736	Thomas Chitter	1774	Thomas Maidman
1737	Joseph Barnard	1775	Richard Whitehead
1738	John Howard	1776	Thomas Parkinson
1739	John Coleman	1777	John Smith
1740	Charles Fairchild	1778	John Wellings
1741	Simon Parsons (died October, 1741)	1779	Joseph Garth
		1780	William Reeves
——	David Lewis	1781	John Foster
1742	John Leech	1782	Thomas Nevett
1743	John Bentley	1783	John Barnard
1744	George Walker	1784	Henry Nash
1745	Robert Miles	1785	John Hatchett
1746	John Halls	1786	Thomas Collingridge
1747	John Cross	1787	John Holyoak
1748	Edward Harlee	1788	William Leader
1749	Joseph Berry	1789	James Marriott
1750	William Trigg	1790	Joseph Bradshaw
1751	Daniel Cogdell	1791	John Foster
1752	William Chapman (resigned "thro want of health" July, 1753)	1792	William Tesse Campbell
		1793	Lionel Lukin
		1794	Arthur Windus
——	John Leech	1795	Edward Berry
1753	William Robins	1796	George Myers
1754	Edward Story	1797	John Wilson
1755	Stephen Hunt	1798	David Stoddart (died August, 1799)
1756	Richard Hodges		
1757	John Rawlins	——	Thomas Collingridge
1758	John Stanley	1799	George Wellings

1800	John Lycet	1841	Benjamin Waller, jun.
1801 1802	William Birch	1842	James Scoles
		1843	James Bennett, jun.
1803	George Eades	1844	George Chancellor
1804	Murdoch Mackenzie	1845	Solomon Willoughby
1805	John Sargeaunt	1846	Thomas Peters
1806	John Randall	1847	John Cook
1807	Osborn Erswell	1848	George Crockford
1808	Samuel May	1849	Henry Black
1809	Edward Houlditch	1850	Lewis James Leslie
1810	Edward William Windus	1851	William Allen Lee
1811	Samuel Jemmett	1852	Thomas Nickalls White
1812	Thomas Bromfield	1853	Thomas Rowley
1813	Anthony Harvey	1854	Thomas Pearce
1814	William Exall	1855	Thomas Mason
1815	John Thomas Rigge	1856	Jehoshophat York
1816	Charles Bonner (resigned April, 1817)	1857	Joseph Glover
		1858	John Winpenny Peters
——	Thomas Titterton	1859	Frederick William Messer
1817	Thomas Titterton	1860	William Winpenny Peters
1818	Osborn Erswell, jun.	1861	Thomas William Callow
1819	Charles Baxter	1862	Joseph Peters
1820	Booth Hancock	1863	Col. James Peters
1821	Samuel Sproston	1864	Thomas How
1822	Luke Hopkinson	1865	William Thomas Thorn
1823	Thomas Windus	1866	James Heslop Powell
1824	Edward William Austin	1867	James Joseph Blake
1825	James Scoles	1868	Charles James Bennett
1826	Benjamin Godfrey Windus	1869	Samuel Glover
1827	Charles Lucas Birch	1870	James Robinson
1828	John Wingfield	1871	John Francis Woodall
1829	Thomas Glover	1872	Herbert Mountford Holmes
1830	James Bennett		
1831	Francis Lamb	1873	John Holland
1832	John Strickland Rigge	1874	George Norgate Hooper
1833	Benjamin Walker the elder	1875	William Hooper
1834	Lewis Leslie	1876	Charles Greenwood
1835	Allen Blizzard	1877	Charles Saunderson
1836	Richard Turrill	1878	Frederic Chancellor
1837	Henry Powell	1879	Charles Dyer Field
1838	Joseph John Scoles	1880	Frederick James Blake
1839	John Chancellor	1881	Frederick Thorn
1840	Thomas Chancellor	1882	William Coham Turner

1883	George Athelstane Thrupp	1912	William Palmer Wilton
1884	Charles Harris Woodall	1913	Sir Joseph Lawrence, Bart.
1885	Henry Rogers	1914	Charles James Bennett
1886	Robert Alford	1915	Thomas Henry Gardiner
1887	Thomas Packwood Alder	1916	John Philipson
1888	Charles Thomas Bartlett	1917	The Rev. Honyel Gough Rosedale, D.D.
1889	William Bristow, Col.		
1890	Alfred Aurelius Clark	1918	Spencer Bernard Kendall
1891	Edmund Boulnois, M.P.	1919	James Fuller Eberle, O.B.E.
1892 1893	{ Sir John Braddick Monckton – Town Clerk of City of London, 1873–1902	1920	Charles Roland Field
		1921	Henry Percival Monckton
		1922	James Leslie Grove Powell
1894	William Beriah Brook	1923	Francis Temple Stowe
1895	Sir Walter Wilkin – Lord Mayor	1924	Francis Danford Thomas
		1925	Clifford Blackburn Edgar
1896	John William Lee, Col.	1926	Arthur Hungerford Pollen
1897	Sir Gainsford Bruce, M.P. for Finsbury 1888–92; Judge of the King's Bench, 1892–1904	1927	Sir Walter Schroder, K.B.E.
		1928	William James McCormack
		1929	Sir Edward Manville
		1930	William Lawton-Goodman
1898	George Edwards		
1899	Robert Downs	1931	Sydney Norris
1900	Francis Joseph Stowe (formerly Stohwasser)	1932	H.R.H. Prince Arthur of Connaught, K.G. etc.
1901	Albert Chancellor	1933	Sir John Davenport Siddely, C.B.E. (cr. Baron Kenilworth, 1937)
1902	Arthur William Elam		
1903	Charles Holmes		
1904	Sir Alfred Seale Haslam, M.P., Newcastle-under-Lyme, 1900–06	1934	Sir Herbert Austin, K.B.E. (cr. Baron Austin of Longbridge, 1936)
		1935	John Christopher Mitchell
1905	Charles Mallord William Turner	1936	Lord Iliffe of Yattendon, C.B.E.
1906	Frederic Wykeham Chancellor, Capt.	1937	Augustus Edward Hughes
		1938	Peter Croall
1907	Robert Greenwood Alford	1939	Algernon Lionel Collins
1908	Ernest William White, Prof.	1940	Vincent Alford
		1941	Douglas Harris, Capt.
1909	Arthur Felton Mulliner, Lt.-Col.	1942	Deputy Charles Gordon Dickson
1910	Arthur Strachan Winterbotham	1943	Sir Frederick Handley-Page, C.B.E.
1911	Frank Lindsay Sutton	1944	Sir William Letts, K.B.E.

1945	James Donald Field	1961	Col. Graham Alexander Norris, O.B.E.
1946	Charles Wilfrid Mallord Turner	1962	Peter Shaw Croall
1947	Archibald Hair	1963	Lt.-Col. Richard Travis Harris
1948	Arthur Conway Edgar, M.C.	1964	Alderman Sir James Miller, G.B.E.
1949	William Macdonald Park	1965	Patrick Norman Dickson
1950	Frederic Stanley Bennett	1966	Hubert Granville Starley, C.B.E.
1951	Richard Melsome Woolley, Major, C.B.E.	1967	Henry John Robert Stent
1952	Edward Philip Connolly	1968	Col. George Douglas Travis Harris, O.B.E.
1953	Roland Edmund Dangerfield	1969	The Rt. Hon. Lord Kenilworth
1954	Wilfrid John Connolly	1970	Sir George Dowty
1955	Group Capt. Frederick Charles Victor Laws, C.B., C.B.E.	1971	Cmdr. Kenneth Anderson Sellar, D.S.O., D.S.C.
1956	Col. The Rt. Hon. Lord Kenilworth, O.B.E.	1973	Paul Kerr Jennens
1957 1958	Ralph James Dalziel Smith	1974	Sir Theo Constantine, C.B.E.
1959	The Hon. Denis (Gomer) Berry	1975	Charles William Ward
1960	Sir (William) Reginald Verdon Smith	1976	Maurice Armstrong Smith, D.F.C.

CLERKS

1677	George Daggett	1915	Henry Smith
1685	Richard Cheslyn junr.	1916	Thomas Henry Gardiner
1690	Brian Courthope	1924	Henry Smith
1693	John Jacob	1934	Benjamin Rhodes Armitage
1718	John Tovey		
1760	Robert Chitter	1942	Ralph James Dalziel Smith
1787	Samuel Collingridge	1942	Frederick Milward Marston (Acting Clerk)
1827	George William Killett Potter (Secondary)	1946	Ralph James Dalziel Smith
1871	George Hillyer	1957	Ralph Bonnett (Acting Clerk)
1871	Jabez Tepper		
1872	Henry Nicholson	1959	Ralph James Dalziel Smith
1887	Peter de Launde Long	1972	Antony Turnbull Langdon-Down
1904	Thomas Henry Gardiner		

Appendix C:
The Company's Arms

Extract from Grant of Arms, 17th July, 29 Charles II 1677

FOR the Arms—Azure a Chevron betwixt three coaches or. For their Crest upon a wreath of their colours—a Phœbus in his glory sitting in his Chariot or drawn through a Cloud proper by four horses argent housed reined and bridled or. And for the Supporters, two horses argent bridled and harnessed sable, the harness studded or garnished gules and housed azure with fringe and purfling or—adorned also with plumes of Feathers or azure argent and gules and this motto at the bottom of the Shield: "Surgit post Nubila Phœbus" as in the margin hereof is more plainly to be seen. And for their Common Seal the Arms above expressed vizt: A Chevron betwixt three Coaches with this circumscription: "Sigillum Commune Societatis opificum Rhedarum et Stratorum London."

Appendix D:
Historical Transport Museums

Bristol City Museum,
   Queens Road, Bristol,
   BS8 1RL, Avon.

Dodington Carriage Museum,
   Dodington, Chipping Sodbury,
   BS17 6SG, Avon.

Bath Carriage Museum,
   Circus Mews, Bath.

The Shuttleworth Collection,
   Old Warden Aerodrome,
   Biggleswade, Beds.

G. C. Mossman,
   Bury Farm, Caddington,
   Nr. Luton, Beds.

Museum of English Rural Life,
   The University, Whiteknights
   Park, Reading, Berks.
   RG6 2AG.

Buckinghamshire County
   Museum,
   Church Street, Aylesbury,
   Bucks.

Gawsworth Hall,
   Macclesfield, Cheshire.

Stockton Transport Museum,
   Preston Park, Yarm Road,
   Stockton, Cleveland.

Museum of Lakeland Life and
   Industry,
   Abbot Hall, Kendall, Cumbria.

Arlington Court,
   Nr. Barnstaple, North Devon.

Buckland Abbey,
   Nr. Yelverton, Devon.

Cheltenham Art Gallery &
   Museum,
   Clarence Street, Cheltenham,
   Glos. GL50 3JT.

North Western Museum of
   Science & Industry,
   97, Grosvenor Street,
   Manchester, M1 6HF,
   Greater Manchester

Breamore Carriage Museum,
   Breamore House,
   Nr. Fordingbridge, Hants.

St. Albans City Museum,
   St. Albans, Herts.

Hull Transport Museum,
   36 High Street,
   Kingston-upon-Hull,
   Humberside.

Scunthorpe Museum & Art
   Gallery,
   Oswald Road, Scunthorpe,
   Humberside, DN15 7BD.

Tyrwhitt-Drake Museum of
  Carriages,
  Archbishop's Stables,
  Mill Street, Maidstone, Kent.

The Royal Umpire Exhibition,
  Croston, Nr. Leyland, Lancs.

Museum of Lincolnshire Life,
  Burton Road, Lincoln.

Gunnersbury Park Museum,
  London, W3 8LQ.

London General Cab Co.
  Museum,
  1–3 Brixton Road, London,
  SW9 6DJ.

London Museum,
  Kensington Palace, W8

Royal Mews,
  Buckingham Palace, SW1

Science Museum,
  Exhibition Road,
  South Kensington, London,
  SW1 2DD.

Hampton Court Palace,
  Middx.

Merseyside County Museum,
  William Broan Street,
  Liverpool 3, Merseyside.

Caister Castle Motor Museum,
  Caister-on-Sea,
  Nr. Gt. Yarmouth, Norfolk.

Sandringham Museums,
  Sandringham Estate, Norfolk.

Nottingham City Museum &
  Art Gallery,
  The Castle, Nottingham,
  NG1 6EL.

The White House Museum of
  Building & Country Life,
  Aston Munslow, Shropshire.

Staffordshire County Museum &
  Mansion House,
  Shugborough, Nr. Stafford.

East Anglia Transport Museum,
  Chapel Road, Carlton Colville,
  Lowestoft, Suffolk.

Cobham Bus Museum,
  Redhill Road, Cobham,
  Surrey, KT11 1EF.

Farnham Museum,
  38 West Street, Farnham,
  Surrey.

Heathfield Wildlife Park,
  Hailsham Road,
  Old Heathfield, East Sussex.

Herbert Art Gallery & Museum,
  Jordan Well, Coventry, Warks.

The Black Country Museum,
  Tipton Road, Dudley, Worcs.

Castle Howard,
  North Yorkshire.

York Castle Museum,
  Tower Street, York,
  North Yorkshire.

Yorkshire Museum of Horse
    Drawn Transport,
    York Mills, Aysgarth Falls,
    Nr. Hawes, North Yorkshire.

Leeds City Museum,
    Municipal Buildings, Leeds,
    West Yorkshire.

The Tolson Memorial Museum,
    Ravensknowle Park,
    Wakefield Road, Huddersfield,
    West Yorkshire.

West Yorkshire Folk Museum,
    Shibden Hall, Shibden Park,
    Halifax, West Yorkshire.

Edinburgh City Transport
    Museum,
    Shrubhill Depot, Leith Walk,
    Lothian.

Glasgow Museum of Transport,
    25 Albert Drive, Glasgow,
    G41 2PE, Strathclyde.

Transport Museum,
    Belfast, Northern Ireland.

Appendix E:
London Taverns Used

Below are the names of localities of London taverns (with Sion College and the Long Room at Hampstead) which were used as meeting places for the binding of apprentices, or on occasion for the assembly of Courts, in the 17th- and 18th-centuries.

Name	Address	Date
Ball	Cow Lane	1678
Bedford Head Tavern	Southampton St., Covent Garden	1749
Black Horse	Bedford Bury	1680
Bufaloes Head Tavern	Bloomsbury Square	1748
Bull	Dean St., Soho	1770
Bull's Head	St. Martin's Lane	1680
Castle Tavern	Without Cripplegate	1754
Ditto ditto	Drury Lane	1736
Coach & Horses	Hanover St., Long Acre	1737
Crosse Keys & Rummer	Henrietta St., Covent Garden	1756
Crown & Septer	St. Martins Lane	1680
Crown Tavern	Bloomsbury	1737
Crowne	against Sargeant's Inne	1677
Dog Tavern	St. Jame's Market	1709
Eagle & Stone	Holborne	1679
Feathers Tavern	against St. Clements Church, Strand	1753
Fox and Goose	near the Three Cranes, Thames Street	1677
George's Coffee House	Haymarket	1705
Globe	Chancery Lane	1680
Ditto Tavern	Strand	1763
Gloucester Tavern	Pall Mall	1739
Golden Ball	Cow Lane	1679
Ditto Dragon	Cow Lane	1677
Haunch of Vension [*sic*]	Lower Brook St.	1764
Hercules Pillars	Gt. Queen St., Lincolns Inn Fields	1780
Hoop Tavern	Leicester feilds	1710
Horn Tavern	Fleet St.	1761
Jackson's Coffee House	Upper Brook St.	1768
King's Armes & One Tun Tavern	The Strand	1746

Name	Address	Date
Kings Arms Tavern	St. Pauls Churchyard	1723
Kings Head Tavern	Broad St., St. Gyles	1763
Long Room	Hampstead—(for Election dinner)	1784
Lunt's Coffee-house		1691
Merry Andrew	Shandos Streete	1678
Morocco Inn	near Soho Square	1704
Prince of Orange's Head Tavern	Jermyn Street	1754
Queens Head Tavern	Great Queen Street	1746
Roe Buck	Bow St., Covent Garden	1729
Rose	over against Furnivall's Inn, near Holborne Barrs	1691
Rummer Tavern	Bishopsgate	1751
,, ,,	Newport Street	1726
,, The	Queen Street	1700
St. Paul's Head Tavern	Cateaton Street, near Guildhall	1737
Salutation	Fish Street	1679
Sion Colledge	London	1678
Standard Tavern	Leicester Fields	1766
Sugar Loaf	Great Queen Street	1710
Sun Tavern	St. Paul's Churchyard	1777
Swan Tavern	King Streete	1680
,, ,,	Smithfield	1707
,, ,,	Old Fish Street	1679
Syder House	Chancery Lane	1680
Three Tuns	Holbourn Bridge	1708
Two Blew Posts Tavern	by Lincoln's Inne Backgate	1730
Turk's Head	Gerrard Street, Soho	1761
Vine Tavern	Holborn	1707
,, ,,	Long Acre	1681–1746
White Hart	Old Bayly	1677
,, Horse	Drury Lane	1680
,, ,,	Purple Lane	1764
,, ,, Alehouse	Drury Lane	1767
,, Lyon	on the backside of Guildhall	1680

Bibliography

A Treatise on Carriages, 1794, William Felton.
Boswell's Life of Johnson, 1791.
Pepys Diary, 1825.
Verney Memoirs, 1892–99.
Kilvert's Diary, 1938–40.
Sophie in London, 1786, Sophie von La Roche.
Annals of the Road, 1876, Captain Malet.
The History of Coaches, 1877, George Thrupp.
Life in a Noble Household, 1937, Scott Thompson.
Travel in England in the Seventeenth Century, 1968, Joan Parkes.
Inventory of Historical Monuments in London, 1929.
The Second World War, 1949, Winston S. Churchill.
The Elegant Carriage, 1961, Marylian Watney.
London's Guilds and Liveries, 1971, John Kennedy Melling.
The Royal Mews, Buckingham Palace, 1975.
Harness, 1882, John Philipson. (New Impression, 1971).
The Art and Craft of Coachmaking, 1897, John Philipson.

In addition, the following appear in the bibliography provided by
Mrs. Watney in her book *The Elegant Carriage*.

English Pleasure Carriages, 1837, W. Bridges Adams.
The Book of the Horse, 1874, S. Sidney.
Coaching, with Anecdotes of the Road, 1876, Lord William Pitt Lennox.
A Practical Treatise on Coachbuilding, 1881, J. W. Burgess.
The Technicalities of the Art of Coachbody Making, 1885, John Philipson.
Highways and Horses, 1888, Athol Maudslay.
Driving, 1889 (Badminton Library), The Duke of Beaufort.
Driving for Pleasure, 1897 (New York), Francis T. Underhill.
The Art and Craft of Coachbuilding, 1897, J. W. Burgess.
Omnibuses and Cabs, 1902, Henry Charles Moore.
Early Carriages and Roads, 1903, Sir Walter Gilbey, Bt.
Driving, 1904 (New York), Francis M. Ware.
Modern Carriages, 1905, Sir Walter Gilbey, Bt.
The Highway and its Vehicles, 1926, Hilaire Belloc.
The English Carriage, 1948, Hugh McCausland.
A Century and a Half of Amateur Driving, 1955–60, A. B. Shone.

BIBLIOGRAPHY

By arrangement with the National Motor Museum at Beaulieu a collection of old books and drawings, the property of the Worshipful Company of Coachmakers & Coach Harnessmakers and the Norris Collection of coachmaking literature, may be examined.

229

Acknowledgements

THE editor would like to thank the following individuals and companies who gave their permission for original drawings, photographs and paintings to be used in reproduction of the illustration plates:

A. J. Newnham (Plate 4); Marylian Watney, author of *The Elegant Carriage* (Plates 5, 6, 12, 15, 21 and 38); Keystone Press Agency Limited (Plates 8 and 24); *Autocar* (Plates 13, 14, 17, 22, 25, 26 and 28); Perfecta Publications Limited (Plate 19); *The Scotsman* Publications Limited (Plate 23); *Flight International* (Plates 27 and 31); *Motor* (Plate 37) and John Richards, Horse-drawn Carriages Limited (Plate 48).

Thanks are also extended to the Harewood Carriage Company Limited and Ashton Keynes Vintage Restorations at whose premises Plates 39 to 46 were photographed.

Permission was kindly given by Cassell & Company Limited to reproduce the extract from *The Second World War* by Winston Churchill on page 85. Acknowledgement is given to the estate of F. R. Fletcher, the editor, for the extracts from *Kilvert's Diary* (Jonathan Cape) on pp 102–104, and to A. D. Peters & Company Limited for the extract from *The Fountain Overflows* by Rebecca West (Macmillan) on pp 129–132.

Other material was supplied by various members of the Coachmakers' Company and from the Company's own archives. In particular, the editor would like to thank Anthony Langdon-Down, the present Clerk of the Company, for his help and encouragement throughout the preparation of this book.

Index

231

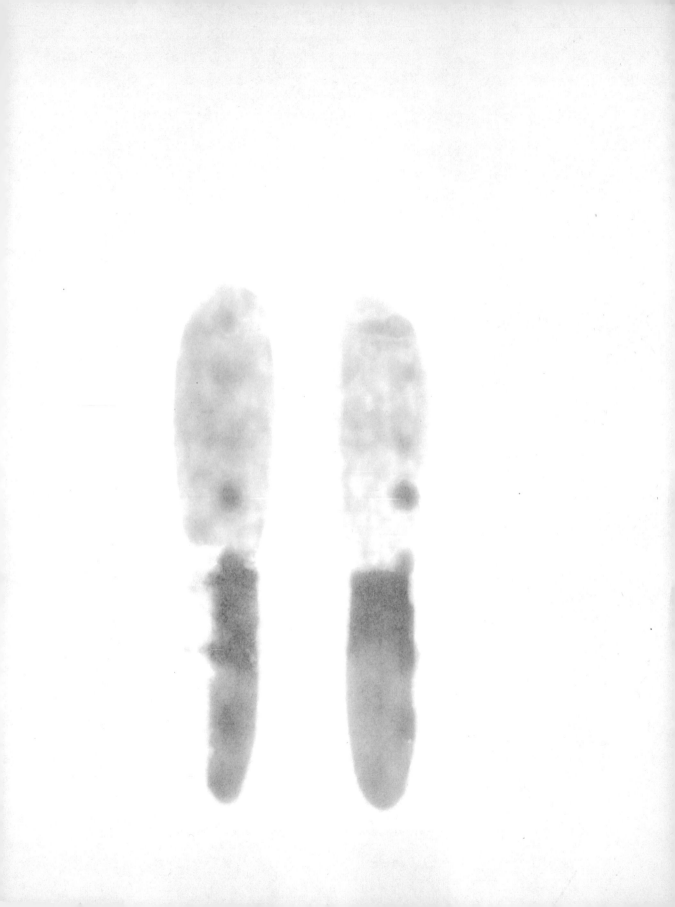